PAM ALLYN & ERNEST MORRELL

EVERY CHILD A SUPER READER

7 Strengths to Open
a World of Possible

SCHOLASTIC

In memory of my father, Bill Krupman.
You are still here with me. This book is for you.
—P. A.

To my three super readers, Amani,
Antonio, and Tripp Morrell.
—E. M.

Credits

Cover photos ©: boy: Mike Kemp Images/Getty Images; book: Veniamin Kraskov/Shutterstock, Inc.

Excerpt from Justice Sonia Sotomayor interview originally broadcast on NPR's *Fresh Air* with Terry Gross, January 13, 2014. Reprinted by permission of WHYY, Inc. *Fresh Air* with Terry Gross is produced at WHYY in Philadelphia and distributed by NPR. Podcasts are available at www.npr.org/podcasts and at iTunes.

My Brother Charlie. Text copyright © 2010 by Holly Robinson Peete and Ryan Elizabeth Peete. Illustrations copyright © 2010 by Shane W. Evans. Reproduced by permission of Scholastic Inc.

Salsa Stories. Copyright © 2000 by Lulu Delacre. Reproduced by permission of Scholastic Inc.

Those Shoes. Text copyright © 2007 by Maribeth Boelts. Illustrations copyright © 2007 by Noah Z. Jones. Reproduced by permission of Candlewick Press, Somerville, MA.

Freak the Mighty. Copyright © 1993 by Rodman Philbrick. Cover art by David Shannon. Reproduced by permission of Scholastic Inc.

Bobby the Brave (Sometimes). Text copyright © 2010 by Lisa Yee. Illustrations copyright © 2010 by Dan Santat. Reproduced by permission of Scholastic Inc.

Just Juice. Text copyright © 1998 by Karen Hesse. Illustrations copyright © 1998 by Robert Andrew Parker. Cover photograph by Bill Bennet/FPG International. Reproduced by permission of Scholastic Inc.

March On! The Day My Brother Martin Changed the World. Text copyright © 2008 by Christine King Farris. Illustrations copyright © 2008 by London Ladd. Reproduced by permission of Scholastic Inc.

Cover Design: Brian LaRossa
Interior Design: Maria Lilja
Interior photographs and video: Monet Izabeth Eliastam
Interior typeset in Aptifer, designed by Mårten Thavenius
Publisher/Acquiring Editor: Lois Bridges
Editor-in-Chief/Development Editor: Raymond Coutu
Editorial Director: Sarah Longhi
Copy Editor: Danny Miller

Copyright © 2016 by Pam Allyn and Ernest Morrell
All rights reserved. Published by Scholastic Inc.
Printed in the U.S.A.

ISBN-13: 978-0-545-94871-5 • ISBN-10: 0-545-94871-1

13 12 11 10   23   25 24 23 22 21 20 19

CONTENTS

Acknowledgments

Ernest and Pam are grateful for the generosity of spirit of Scholastic. We thank Lois Bridges, the editor of a lifetime, for her expansive, child-centered vision, integrity, and expertise; Ray Coutu, our genius development editor, who made it all happen with pure magic; Sarah Longhi, luminous editorial director; and Danny Miller, our brilliant copy editor. Thanks to Brian LaRossa for his masterful art direction and to Maria Lilja for her beautiful interior design. None of this would have been possible without the leadership of Billy DiMichele, Greg Worrell, and the great Dick Robinson. Gratitude to the exceptional Dorothy Lee and to our LitWorld and LitLife colleagues, led by amazing Carolyn Greenberg and the team of Rebekah Coleman, Talia Kovacs, Brian Johnson, David Wilcox, Aimee Deutsch, Diandra Malahoo, Monica Burns (superhero tech star!), Megan Karges, Jennifer Estrada, Ana Stern, Yohanna Briscoe, Amber Peterson, Yaya Yuan, Leah Joseph, and Brooke Stone. A special thanks to Debbie Lera, whose care, wisdom, and values touch every page. Thanks to LitWorld's Board of Directors: Ellen Fredericks, Sue Atkins, Sabrina Conyers, Sophie Belisha, Julie Hirschfeld, Lauren Blum, Chernor Bah, Nicole Nakashian, Donna Stein, Christine Chao, and Jeff DaPuzzo. To Monet Eliastam who brings our work to visual life, the children of the Port Chester and Wooster Schools, and the wonderful teachers there, too. Our abundant gratitude to all the children with whom we work.

Pam thanks her communities of love and support. She is grateful for the inspiration of teacher colleagues, especially Rose Mureka, sister of her heart. With gratitude to Mike Lavington and Paul Blum for conversations about innovation. So grateful for Jim, Katie and Charlotte, and Anne, Cindy and Lou, for every blessed moment. With appreciation for Sue Meigs, for our friendship and for the care she gives to the readers who need us most. Pam is thankful for the authors who wrote the books that changed her life: E. B. White, Langston Hughes, Lucy Maud Montgomery, Zora Neale Hurston, Naomi Shihab Nye. With love, now and forever.

Ernest thanks the administrators, professors, and students at Teachers College, Columbia University, for their passion for literacy and their commitment to urban education. He's indebted to President Susan Fuhrman, Provost Tom James, and his colleagues in the English Education program: Sheridan Blau, Ruth Vinz, Janet Miller, Yolanda Sealey Ruiz, and Bob Fecho. Ernest is also indebted to his team at the Institute for Urban and Minority Education (IUME) for its tireless advocacy for research and practice in city schools and after-school programs, and for its amazing work with young people, which has inspired many of the ideas in this book. A special thanks to Veronica Holly, Sandra Overo, and to the faculty, postdoctoral fellows, and graduate students who make IUME possible. Finally, Ernest would like to thank his partner in crime of 22 years, Dr. Jodene Morrell, for the ongoing conversation that is children's literacy and their collaborative professional crusade.

FOREWORD

We at the Children's Defense Fund (CDF) have long believed that reading is an indispensable key to unlocking the door to children's dreams and unlimited potential. Our CDF Freedom Schools® program is grounded in a literature-rich environment and reading curriculum centered on excellent books that reflect a wide variety of cultures, races, and experiences. For some children, it is the first time they have seen books with characters who look like them. Our goal is to help children fall in love with reading, so much so they respond with comments such as, "I enjoyed learning about my history." "That [book] really inspired me because he came from a rough neighborhood." "Freedom Schools taught me when I learn, I can have fun with it. It made me a better reader because I can understand things." "I see myself, and the books give me hope."

All children deserve to fall in love with the power of the written word to transport them to new worlds and teach them new ideas, and to experience what writer Pat Mora has called *bookjoy*. Yet too many children miss out on that opportunity. In fact, far too many children cannot read at all. The majority of all children in the United States and nearly three-quarters of our Black and Latino children can't read at grade level. They are being sentenced to social and economic death in our rapidly globalizing world. A 21-year-old student teacher described the connection between an inability to read and entrapment in our nation's dangerous pipeline to prison: "If you can't read by third grade, you don't want anyone to know you can't read, so you act out. When you act out, you get grouped with the other kids who act out. They can't read [either]. Because no one can read and no one discusses that they can't read, they end up becoming part of gangs, and everyone there is there for the same reason."

No child deserves to have the doors to the "world of possible" slammed shut. So I am profoundly grateful for this new book. In *Every Child a Super Reader,* Pam Allyn and Dr. Ernest Morrell share lessons that will help educators and parents everywhere enable more children to become proficient readers. Their book shows how developing every child's confidence, courage, and hope is vital for learning; showcases the transformational power of literacy in a child's life; describes how to create the kinds of safe and supportive learning environments that exclude no child; promotes equity, opportunity, and the chance for every child to be heard; embraces multicultural children's literature and the power of storytelling as a pathway to academic, social, and civic development; and connects the in-school work of literacy education to homes, families, and out-of-school contexts in order to immerse children in a rich, joyful, literate environment brimming with books and conversation about books 365 days a year.

We *can* create this world for all our children. *Every Child a Super Reader* provides a blueprint for nurturing the engaged and fluent readers we want all of our children to be. In the process, we will transform children's lives and life chances.

—**MARIAN WRIGHT EDELMAN**
President, Children's Defense Fund

INTRODUCTION

THIS CHILD IS A SUPER READER

"For these are all our children."
—JAMES BALDWIN

You know this child. She is wearing her superhero outfit, with cape and goggles, hair sticking up. She's running around the playground, powered by sheer joy and believing 1,000 percent she can change the world.

You also know this child. He sits in the back of the classroom, dreaming his dreams, wishing for a bigger, stronger, bolder voice. Although he wants his ideas to be heard, he does not raise his hand.

And you know this child, too—the one moving more slowly than her classmates, preoccupied, a lot on her mind, her backpack burgeoning, spilling papers.

All children are full of hopes and dreams. Yet too often challenges get in their way. The school day can be long and hard for them, and time out of school can be even longer and harder.

How can we truly tap into the superpowers inside each and every child? How can we create a world for children in which they can raise their voices and become empowered as readers, writers, and thinkers? How can we tap into children's strengths—strengths that make them strong, confident, and curious during class, during out-of-school time, and back at home? By bringing out the super reader within them.

Super reading transforms, exhilarates, provokes, and inspires. It is the kind of reading that empowers children to feel at ease in any setting, to explore, to share ideas. It is the kind of reading that changes children's lives and, by doing so, changes the world.

For that to happen, though, we need to offer children "surround sound" reading. We need to give them the time and space to read like a super reader every day of the week, every week of the month, every month of the year, in school and out of school. By focusing on their strengths, we help them build a super reader life.

Super readers have questions that light fires within them. They understand the complexities of a problem and embrace them. Yet too many children never receive the kind of teaching that brings out the super reader within them. Let's change that right now. This is our time. All children can and should be empowered by reading because reading is, by its very nature, empowering.

> "We need to offer children 'surround sound' reading. We need to give them the time and space to read like a super reader every day of the week, every week of the month, every month of the year, in school and out of school."

Let us teach every child how to live like a reader and to use reading as a superpower to elevate her mind, spirit, and overall sense of well-being. Through the gift of reading, we give this child the chance to be in the world—a world that she makes her own, where she never feels alone, 365 days a year.

When we raise and teach a super reader, we are not simply showing him how to decode at the speed of light, or turn pages quickly, or finish a book in record time (though those may be by-products of raising and teaching super readers). We are teaching him how to become a reader. How to live like a reader. We must always remember, reading is not only about what the child does when he reads, but also what reading does for the child.

Reading today is about reading widely and voluminously across many media, genres, and experiences. Reading online or print text is not an either/or paradigm. Children are growing up in a complex, blended world where reading in every mode and on multiple platforms is more essential than ever. We must embrace that fact if we want children to become super readers. If we want them to experience the visceral joy and power of reading.

This book will help you create the kind of strength-based communities that build a hunger and passion for reading. It will help you to create environments that honor choice and voice in the child's reading life and to create easy-to-implement structures that make it possible for all of us, as teachers, out-of-school educators, and parents, to unleash the child's inner super reader.

The super reader is powered by sheer joy, by a feeling of belonging to a reading community, by her own strengths, and by an understanding of the power of those strengths.

Consider this book a call to action to launch a super reader community, from school to after school to home and back again. A community in which we all raise our voices, hearts, and minds to help every child become a super reader who can change the world—and will.

Why This Book?

Whether you're a classroom teacher, out-of-school educator, reading specialist, literacy coach, librarian, or school administrator, this book gives you the information and inspiration you need to turn all children into super readers.

Our goal is to help you create an equitable and richly accessible reading community, where every child can learn the skills of reading and feel safe taking risks as a reader.

Foundational skills, such as decoding, gaining phonemic awareness, and learning academic vocabulary, are crucial to the child's reading process, but they must be taught within a purposeful context. Children need to be taught why it's important to read—and have clear reasons to read—if they're going to learn how to read well. It is that purposeful context that has been missing in many of our classrooms and out-of-school programs, and so we address it head-on in this book.

The 7 Strengths Model, described in Chapter 2, helps you build that context. It recognizes the child's social-emotional development as an essential, often overlooked key to successful reading outcomes. Our social-emotional framework—created with children's intra- and inter-personal skills at its heart—builds a safe and loving environment in which to cultivate forever-learners who are excited and ready for their futures in a college, career, and civic life.

The model is an asset-based, strength-based model that centers on what children can do. It relies on children's understandings of themselves as learners, high-quality children's literature, and the research-based benefits of social-emotional learning. When children:

- feel a sense of belonging in a community of readers
- satisfy curiosity through literature and informational texts
- form meaningful friendships that provide support for learning
- learn kindness to reach out to other readers and be world-changers
- develop confidence to get through the hard parts of reading
- build courage for risk-taking in literacy learning
- cultivate a spirit of hopeful optimism for achievement of reading goals

they are far more likely to become super readers who can read across platforms, across genres, in any circumstance, and for any purpose.

The California Department of Education created a set of standards for English learners. In part, it reads:

> *Offer students opportunities to interact deeply, as readers and writers, with a range of high-quality texts—different types, genres, topics, disciplines, lengths, and complexities—that ignite their interests, build their knowledge, touch their hearts, and illuminate the human experience* (2015).

This vision sets us on a path to a new era—an era in which we ignite interests, build knowledge, touch hearts, and illuminate the human experience. This is what we want for all children, for they deserve nothing less. The deficit-oriented labels we have historically given children have long-lasting, detrimental effects. Instead of talking about super readers, we have talked more about "problem readers," "struggling readers," and even "non-readers." Instead of talking about a world of possible, we have talked about barriers to reading achievement.

Too many children are not thriving as readers in school or out of school. Research shows that children who are reading below level by third grade are four times as likely to drop out of high school than those who have reached proficiency. While reading scores in general are low across the country, children from low-income households make up nearly 75 percent of the population reading below the 25th percentile (Reardon, 2011).

Learning to Read: What Every Child Needs

Learning to read is typically defined as learning to control a specific set of skills. And while it's certainly true that children must learn to orchestrate a complex set of strategic actions that enable comprehension and decoding, it's equally true that learning to read is a social-cultural event. In other words, learning to read is more than simple skill building. Children also become readers when they are immersed in a community of readers, surrounded by rich book talk and animated demonstrations of reading, and provided with the social-emotional support that enables them to become members of the "literacy club" (Smith, 1987). Thus, at the same time we're helping students acquire the technical skills necessary for proficient reading, we also work to help children develop the confidence to take the risks needed to propel learning forward. Learning to read, like any human endeavor, requires practice, perseverance, and persistence to push through the challenges to proficiency.

One reason many children are not thriving as readers is that they have come to see themselves through their perceived deficits. You know these children. They are the ones who are too often pulled out for remediation just as we begin that beautiful read aloud or invite the other children to join us in a rich, whole-class reading experience.

This book is about how we can change the paradigm from deficit to strength. We are entering an age of participatory education in which everyone's voices should and can matter—including children's. We offer a different way to think about all children as readers, one that starts with the possible.

You'll close this book understanding:

- The hope and vision for what a super reader is and can be.

- The benefits of strength-based instruction using the 7 Strengths Model.

- The indispensable powers of reading and why every child should have them.

- The practical in-school and out-of-school strategies for helping all children become 365-day super readers.

- The formative assessments that allow you to measure to what extent students are grasping the big ideas they need to be successful.

Join us now to help the children in your life become super readers.

How This Book Is Organized

Every Child a Super Reader gives you all the background information you need to understand why our model works so well for children—and all the tools you need to implement the model. Chapter 1 explores the benefits of super reading and principles that undergird the development of super readers. Chapter 2 explains the 7 Strengths Model, the thinking behind it, and the power it holds to create super readers. Chapters 3 to 9 provide in-depth discussions of each strength, as well as strength-specific lessons and family guides. And, finally, Chapters 10 to 14 provide what you need to implement the model effectively—essential practices, assessment tools, and planning guidelines. (Find digital versions of assessment, management, and planning tools, as well as family guides, at scholastic.com/superreaderresources.)

PART I

THE POWER TO CREATE SUPER READERS

The 7 Strengths Model

CHAPTER 1

HOW READING OPENS A WORLD OF POSSIBLE FOR EVERY CHILD

"A capacity, and taste, for reading, gives access to whatever has already been discovered by others. It is the key, or one of the keys, to the already solved problems. And not only so. It gives a relish, and facility, for successfully pursuing the [yet] unsolved ones."

—ABRAHAM LINCOLN

n a recent National Public Radio interview, Supreme Court Justice Sonia Sotomayor recounted a transformational experience from her first year in college:

One day talking to my first-year roommate… I was telling her about how out of place I felt at Princeton, how I didn't connect with many of the experiences that some of my classmates were describing, and she said to me, "You're like Alice in Wonderland."

And I said, "Who is Alice?"

And she said, "You don't know about Alice?"

And I said, "No, I don't."

And she said, "It's one of the greatest book classics in English literature. You should read it."

I recognized at that moment that there were likely to be many other children's classics that I had not read. Before I went home that summer, I asked her to give me a list of some of the books she thought were children's classics and she gave me a long list,

and I spent the summer reading them. That was perhaps the starkest moment
of my understanding that there was a world I had missed (2014).

There are so many children in our classrooms and communities like Justice Sotomayor. Children filled with promise but who, for many reasons, have not been given the opportunity to connect to a wide range of literature and reading experiences. Today, this is such an unnecessary tragedy, as we know so much about the joy and power of reading and how to make that joy and power possible for all children, regardless of their life circumstances. Reading opens every child's world.

Super reading impacts every aspect of a child's life: the personal, social, academic, and civic. The child who reads gains comfort, community, and connection to the wider world.

Reading is humankind's greatest innovation, touching all corners of achievement. Reading is the linchpin to success, the foundational goal of all goals. Super reading opens the possibilities for the child to learn and grow as an individual, succeed in academics, connect with others, and become an engaged participant in the civic life of the community.

What Is a "Super Reader"?

The super reader is a child who enters a text with purpose. Regardless of platform (print or digital) and genre (fiction, informational, or poetry), she reads that text with deep comprehension and finishes it feeling satisfied, informed, and inspired. What's more, the super reader can respond to and expound on the text in conversation and writing and use what she learns from the text to make points and answer questions.

 For a video of Pam and Ernest discussing the definition of "super reader," visit scholastic.com /superreaderresources.

The super reader is confident—so confident, in fact, that she is willing to tackle texts that are difficult for her to comprehend. Like a rock climber on a particularly challenging part of a climbing wall, she savors developing strategies that are necessary for her success.

The super reader understands the demands of the text—how, for example, its diagrams, charts, graphs, tables, captions, and other features influence the reading process, as well as structural elements such as table of contents, chapters, headings and subheadings, glossary, and index. She recognizes literary techniques such as flashbacks, foreshadowing, and stories within stories, as well as literary elements such as metaphors, similes, and idioms, and uses them to engage more actively with the text.

The super reader reads voluminously. She connects with an author, embracing, questioning, and challenging his or her ideas. The super reader notices author's craft such as the use of punctuation and the use of white space to add meaning, the tone of the piece, the choices of words and phrases, and the fluid interplay of dialogue and description.

The super reader may read in more than one language. He recognizes his home language as an asset and is willing to share his unique perspective with others with confidence and pride.

The super reader is reflective. She questions herself and the text: "What does it mean for me to become an even better reader?" She is aware of her growth as a reader, setting small and large goals for herself. She understands that becoming a super reader is a continuous process and not an end in itself.

The super reader is a flashlight-in-bed kind of reader, a back-of-the-cereal-box kind of reader, a text-messaging kind of reader, and a comic-book-to-classic-novel kind of reader. And, indeed, the super reader loves to read.

The Benefits of Super Reading

Try to imagine a world without reading. Words—reading them, writing them, speaking them—are so central to how most of the world functions that it is nearly impossible for many of us to comprehend what it would mean to live without them. Now, try to imagine what your life would be like if *you* couldn't read. It would be frightening, isolating, disheartening, frustrating, even paralyzing. You might feel like there is no place for you in the world. As if, in the words of Walt Whitman, "the powerful play goes on, and you will contribute a verse," yet you have no verse to contribute.

As teachers, administrators, and community service providers who care about children and their futures, we know much is at stake. Communication is central to how we function in our society. Our innovations in technology, transportation, education, and business stem from the desire to connect individuals to one another with more efficiency and effectiveness. At the heart of communication lies literacy, the skill that makes it all possible.

And so, too, there are the breathtaking learning benefits of voluminous reading:

- developing extensive vocabularies

- having the skills to navigate different kinds of text

- acquiring analytical problem-solving skills

- understanding how reading works—how to orchestrate innumerable skills and strategies in the drive to make meaning

- understanding how writing works—how to spell, punctuate, and create a logically organized sentence, paragraph, and complete, cohesive piece

Super Reading Translates Into High Achievement

Today, a high school dropout is ineligible for 90 percent of jobs in the United States. With 1.1 million dropouts every year in the U.S. (*Education Week*, 2012), we cannot afford to continue to let children grow up without discovering the life-changing effects of joyful learning and a deep engagement with transformative literature.

Reading is a great equalizer that has the power to break down the typical barriers to education, those invisible walls built around coveted zip codes and elite institutions. In a study of 6,000 16-year-olds, Sullivan and Brown (2013) found that reading for pleasure was a greater influence on a child's vocabulary, math, and spelling scores than whether their parents held degrees. Literacy expert John Guthrie (2004) found that low-income students with high reading engagement routinely excelled over their peers with higher-income and better-educated parents. The research is clear: engaged reading translates into high achievement.

Engagement is also essential for meeting the standards. Voluminous independent reading is the best way to meet the goals the standards establish. Though the standards vary from state to state, reading is at the core of each and every one of them (Allington, Billen, & McCuiston, 2015). Literacy is also a key predictor of children's high school graduation rates and college success.

Super Reading Builds Empathy and Understanding

Reading fiction develops empathy—and there's research to prove it. Djikic, Oatley, and Moldoveanu (2013) found that their research participants who were frequent fiction readers had higher scores on a measure of empathy. The key point is that we can be different; fiction moves us to change. Anne Murphy Paul articulates the power of cognitive scientist Keith Oatley's research in her *New York Times* op-ed, "Your Brain on Fiction":

> Brain scans are revealing what happens in our heads when we read a detailed description, an evocative metaphor, or an emotional exchange between characters. Stories…stimulate the brain and even change how we act in life. (2012)

That's because our brains are, in a sense, fooled—they aren't able to differentiate between the fictional experience and the real-life event. In their research, Kidd and Castano (2013) found that while reading literary fiction, we are forced to use the same mental faculties that help us navigate successful social relationships. When compared with reading nonfiction or no reading at all, groups that read literary fiction were consistently rated as having greater empathy. When we read a narrative through multiple perspectives or infer the thoughts of characters, we are exercising the exact cognitive functions that help us become empathetic beings. These complex relationships and narrative structures are often missing from alternate types of reading material, such as nonfiction and informational texts.

Consider the power of Harry Potter in reducing prejudice. "Results from one experimental intervention and two cross-sectional studies show that reading the Harry Potter novels improves attitudes toward stigmatized groups among those more identified with the main positive character and those less identified with the main negative character." Vezzali et al. (2014) also found that adopting the different perspectives in Harry Potter is a way to foster empathy for marginalized groups such as refugees or other stigmatized groups. In general, reading fiction helps us discover ourselves, expand our understanding of the world—and develop empathy for others.

Reading can help ease the lonely and isolating moments of life, offering comfort in the well-loved passages of an oft returned-to favorite or guidance within the crisp pages of a newly made acquaintance. In talking about what they read with family and friends, young people develop their self and their social identities, navigating their personal journeys through the sometimes choppy waters of gender and ethnicity (Moje et al., 2008).

Reading keeps us company. Great literature accompanies us through our lifetime. A good book can serve as guide, mentor, friend, and companion through our most exhilarating times and through our loneliest of times.

Super Reading Builds Children's Sense of Self and Emotional Resilience

A kinship with books and stories gives children and adults the skills and emotional strength to believe a dream and make it real. Martin Luther King, Jr., was powerfully influenced by the stories in the Bible when writing his speeches and crafting a life of social change. Whenever Joan Didion is ready to begin writing a new book, she first rereads Joseph Conrad's *Victory* because "it makes it seem worth doing."

As a young child growing up on farms in Kentucky, Indiana, and Illinois, Abraham Lincoln was too poor and too busy working to have much time for formal schooling. Yet he became a voracious reader, losing himself in a book whenever and wherever he could. It was often said that he could be seen with a book in one hand and an axe in another. Lincoln's love for reading gave him access to worlds that would not have been otherwise possible for him. He credited his love for reading with helping him to become the 16th president of the United States, and he became one of the greatest leaders and freedom fighters our nation has ever known.

We read "the world" as noted Brazilian educator Paulo Freire (1970) has argued, and we "read the word." We read on tablets, sticky notes, text messages, the backs of napkins. We voraciously read street signs and Google searches. We read notes from a friend that make our hearts leap and memos from a colleague that make us stay up late to finish a project. Reading inspires, provokes, motivates, and frustrates. It accompanies us in our every waking moment if we are lucky, and profoundly marginalizes those who are not able to access it.

Super Reading Prepares Children for the Future… Whatever That Might Be!

As we move at light speed through the information age, reading is increasingly important to our personal, social, academic, and civic lives. The first public schools were formed in the United States at the end of the 19th century because government leaders and educators understood that the world was changing and that literacy skills would be important to our future. As we race toward the middle of the 21st century, this has never been truer. As teachers, family members, caregivers, librarians, and out-of-school providers, it has never been more important for us to work together to cultivate strong and confident readers. Literacy is humankind's greatest innovation because it is so adaptable to new worlds. Whether we're using tablets, smartphones, or printed books, reading paves the way to new discoveries, new opportunities, and new dimensions in learning.

Raising Super Readers: 10 Fundamental Principles

Ten principles undergird the development of super readers.

Principle 1: *Super readers learn to read by reading interactively.*

Reading is a complex activity involving, among other things, decoding of symbols, awareness of the modalities of how stories and information are presented through text, familiarity with vocabulary, and an ability to make literal and metaphoric connections. Effective reading brings all these skills and abilities together to enable us to make meaning from the text.

Not unlike learning to ride a bike, the only way to learn how to draw all these components together in the pursuit of meaning is to dig into text and read—a lot—in school and out.

Everything builds on itself. The adult reading to the child reiterates the flow and power of stories and the emotional connection of reading with comfort and happiness. Work with phonics enables effective decoding and symbolic recognition. School instruction helps focus on the strategies and techniques to make readers stronger and faster. Conversations at home reinforce curiosity and get to the point of why we read. Reading requires daily practice, which is wonderful because it means that we can help kids become super readers every moment of every day.

Principle 2: *Super readers have a strong foundation in oral language.*

Children enter reading with a rich base of linguistic know-how; they understand what language is and how it works. At the same time they are acquiring the technical skills that enable successful reading—with expert teacher guidance—they also need lots and lots of time inside real books, familiarizing themselves with the basics of book handling. All children, especially those who initially find reading challenging, need time to explore real texts and practice reading on their own and with others.

The read aloud plays a powerful role in the 7 Strengths Model. It immerses children in literary and informational language, introducing them to rich, wide-ranging vocabulary they aren't likely to encounter anywhere but through books. The child growing up in a biliterate or multiliterate home or school absorbs the rich linguistic input from the read aloud and transfers it to the work of decoding and meaning making that reading requires.

Talking about texts is essential, too, because it provides additional meaning-making scaffolds. It deepens, extends, and refines the meaning that children absorb through each read aloud—and this is especially key for emerging bilinguals and multilinguals. When children talk about texts or collaborate on ideas about texts, it's a pivotal part of the reading experience. Discourse deepens text understanding. It is a vital part of the super reader's learning process.

Principle 3: *Super readers understand that reading and writing are mutually beneficial language processes.*

Reading is like breathing in and writing is like breathing out. Reading and writing are complex developmental language processes involving the orchestration and integration of a range of understandings, strategies, skills, and attitudes. Both processes develop as natural extensions of children's need to communicate and make sense of their experiences. Every time we enter a text as a reader, we receive a writing lesson: how to spell, punctuate, use grammar, structure a sentence or paragraph, and organize a text. We also learn the many purposes writing serves and the genres and formats it assumes to serve those purposes (Duke, 2014; Culham, 2010).

What seems to distinguish students who succeed from those who don't is the ability to engage independently in a close analysis of demanding text—and there may be no better way to accomplish that goal than through writing. Writing has a strong and consistently positive impact on reading comprehension. The benefits of writing about text are both abundant and profound—and mirror the kind of thinking we want our students to do when they are reading (Graham & Perin, 2007; Graham & Hebert, 2010):

- Engage in deep thinking about ideas.
- Draw on their own knowledge and experience.
- Consolidate and review information.
- Organize and integrate ideas.
- Be explicit about text evidence.
- Be reflective and reformulate thinking.
- Note personal involvement.
- Capture the reading experience in their own words.

Principle 4: *Super readers read broadly and deeply for authentic purposes.*

Super readers are voracious. They are hungry to read and can read easily across many genres. They are absorbing great amounts of words, images, and text of all kinds. They are not daunted by the complexities of genre, the bold headline of an informational text, the white space of a poem, or the dense volume of a novel. All these things delight and intrigue them. They are not afraid because they see the purposes for reading in the world and understand the challenges of reading. They have favorites they devour and books they want to reread. They read a magazine while going to their out-of-school activity, social media to find out what their friends are doing, and a long biography of someone they want to know more about in their free time.

They can navigate the unique complexities of each genre. They have questions they want to answer, puzzles they want to solve, places they want to get to, and they are certain that reading will get them there.

Principle 5: *Super readers have access to many kinds of texts.*

The choices we give to children must be abundant. A child's tastes and interests are changing constantly. Do regular surveys to check in on what children love to read and why. (See page 174 for a survey.) Update the classroom library for your students at least three times a year, introducing new texts, removing texts that are no longer useful, and rearranging how texts are organized. The school and classroom library can and should extend beyond a collection of books and magazines housed on shelves. Digital books, slide shows, and websites and other electronic texts that are available online are valuable resources as well. Set up systems for students to safely and efficiently access digital material.

In addition to typical fiction and information books, have comic books, cookbooks, how-to books, celebrity magazines, books on favorite hobbies, and others. Opportunities to examine photographs, diagrams, infographics, and other visual texts are also very valuable. The number of books and texts the child is exposed to matters a lot. An essential aspect of becoming a super reader is knowing yourself as a reader—made possible through wide reading driven by access to abundant texts and personal choice.

Principle 6: *Super readers need the freedom to make choices about what they read.*

The research on student self-selected reading is robust and conclusive. Students read more, understand more, and are more likely to continue reading when they have the opportunity to choose what they read (Allington & Gabriel, 2012). Choice is inherently connected to engagement. When a child is guided by her own interests, she will be led to material that excites and stimulates her. This engagement with the text is a critical component of a child's education. In a 2014 study of family attitudes and behaviors around reading, 91 percent of children ages 6–17 agreed, "My favorite books are the ones that I have picked out myself" (Scholastic, 2015). A study detailed in *Becoming a Nation of Readers: The Report of the Commission on Reading* (Anderson, Hiebert, Scott, & Wilkinson, 1985) found that: "the 'interestingness' of a text is thirty times more powerful than the readability of text when it comes to comprehension and recall." Nancie Atwell's powerful writing on creating a "literate environment" within her own classrooms shows this in action. By establishing back-and-forth letter writing with her students, Atwell was able to engage in meaningful discussions with each student while also keeping track of their personal thoughts and reading development. Students wrote to Atwell about their frustrations and triumphs, which Atwell would then use to guide them toward texts that might be of use and interest. Even the most reticent of students were finding their own reading material, with confidence and enthusiasm, by the end of the school year (Atwell, 2014).

Each child has unique interests and ideas that will spark his learning journey. As teachers and family members, we must give children the strategies to find texts that will challenge them and the space to grow in the direction they choose. Research shows that when children have more control in choosing their own reading materials, they will select texts that develop their literacy skills—and they will be engaged in the process (Johnson & Blair, 2003). This may mean rereading an old favorite one day and trying something new the next. If a child is taught selection strategies and allowed to explore a diverse library, then whatever he chooses will help him along his learning journey.

Principle 7: *Super readers need "reading role models."*

In addition to helping our students learn to control the specific skills that are necessary for effective reading, we can also help them acquire a deep understanding of what all capable readers do as they work their way through a text. They can see us doing the work of reading with them, from reading aloud to them, to demonstrating close reading to make reading itself visible, to coaching them in their independent reading. We can be more open with students about our own work as readers: building vocabulary and fluency, working on our stamina, and becoming braver and bolder in our growth as readers in what we read throughout the day and in why we make the choices we make. We can share:

- when reading has felt hard for us
- when reading has felt great
- our inner thinking about texts
- what we do when we get to hard parts
- what kinds of choices we make as readers and when
- how we fall in love with authors, genres, and types of text

In general, making visible the strategic actions we employ to guide our own reading is one of the most effective ways to help young readers in our care.

Principle 8: *Super readers thrive in a collaborative community of readers.*

Reading is not solitary. Super readers love to share. And they love to get recommendations and hear what someone else is thinking about a text. Collaboration is about constructing new ideas together about what we read. It is about trusting that the environment is safe for ideas that may not be fully formed but will grow by reading more and more and speaking and listening, too. Speaking and listening are part of the literacy experience, and they are part of how super readers grow.

Principle 9: *Super readers develop the strengths and skills to read by spending time reading independently.*

While targeted small-group reading instruction is essential, giving children time to practice the strategic actions necessary for effective reading is equally essential.

Children who read independently perform better in school (Cullinan, 2000; Hiebert & Reutzel, 2010). According to Cullinan, the more students read in school and out of school, the more gains they demonstrate in reading proficiency. "Among all the ways children spent their time, reading books was the best predictor of several measures of reading achievement, including gains in reading achievement between second and fifth grade" (Anderson et al., 1988). Students with access to rich texts and given time to read independently in and out of school will make great strides (Allington & McGill-Franzen, 2013).

The amount of free reading done outside of school has consistently been found to relate to growth in vocabulary, reading comprehension, verbal fluency, and general information (Anderson, Wilson, & Fielding, 1988; Guthrie & Greaney, 1991; Taylor, Frye, & Maruyama, 1990). Students who read independently become better readers, score higher on achievement tests in all subject areas, and have greater content knowledge than those who do not (Cunningham & Zibulsky, 2014; Krashen, 2004).

Principle 10: *Super readers are joyful readers.*

Pleasure is always at the heart of engaged super reading. Children who read avidly with delight and joy understand themselves as readers, know their own reading interests and passions, and, as a result, are adept at finding the texts that maximize reading pleasure. Super reading programs that invite reading choice and promote reading pleasure give rise to super readers who not only read but also, more importantly, want to read.

Next Steps in the Journey

We hope that by now you are convinced of the need to develop the super reader in every child. But you may be asking yourself, "How do we do this? How can I contribute to this worthy endeavor?" Chapter 2 explains the 7 Strengths Model, the thinking behind it, and the power it holds to create super readers. On with the journey!

THE 7 STRENGTHS MODEL: A NEW WAY TO ENSURE EVERY CHILD'S SUCCESS

"Rather than impose upon your kids or try and steer their lives in a certain direction…recognize what their strengths are and support their strengths and support the development of the things they're passionate about."

—DR. EDWARD ZUCKERBERG,
father of Facebook founder Mark Zuckerberg

This book shines a spotlight on the work we can do as educators, in and out of school, 365 days a year. Time in school and time out of school can build the life of a super reader. Or not, depending on our actions. The 7 Strengths Model is designed to show you the "why" and the "how" of the life of a super reader. It's a flexible, robust, and adaptable model that works during the school day and in any out-of-school experience. The model's social-emotional emphasis ensures children a sense of safety and well-being as readers and access to quality literature that builds lifelong connections to textual experiences and higher-level thinking skills. The 7 Strengths Model connects reading to the inner life of the child, providing a full toolkit for learning to read and reading to learn. The child has to know how reading connects to his deepest experience as a human being. The model starts with what the child brings to school and to out-of-school programs and uses intrinsic human strengths to help that child connect to texts, experience the power of reading, and become confident in taking on everyday challenges as a reader.

In their groundbreaking research, Dick Allington and Anne McGill-Franzen (2013) show that 80 percent of the achievement gap between students of lower- and upper-socioeconomic backgrounds is credited to summer reading loss. By the time a child living in poverty reaches fifth grade, she may have lost the equivalent of three years of education. This in turn affects the entire classroom, as teachers may spend at least a month reteaching students material forgotten over the summer. While the wealthiest strata has recovered from the massive recession of 2008, most of the U.S. hasn't. According to the National Center for Children in Poverty (NCCP), nearly half of U.S. school children are low-income, which is defined as those families living within 200 percent of the federal poverty threshold. It is important to understand that this number of poor and low-income children in America has risen dramatically over the past 15 years, and it is expected to continue to rise in the near future. We now find ourselves with many central city and rural schools and districts where the overwhelming majority of students live in poor and low-income homes and communities.

We do not present these numbers because we are pessimistic about the future or because we feel that poverty is a barrier that we cannot overcome. To the contrary, we have both seen and worked with children and families that have created super readers across every social strata. The 7 Strengths Model takes into account the entirety of a child's reading life, from home to school to out of school and home again.

How the Model Came to Be

We, Pam and Ernest, are founding leaders of LitWorld, an organization that provides transformational literacy experiences for children across the United States and in more than 60 countries. Pam is the Founding Director and Ernest is a member of the Executive Board of Directors. We both lead literacy initiatives across the country in many different kinds of schools (urban, rural, suburban, public, charter, private). In leading literacy work on the ground in New York City, Detroit, Chicago, and then, starting in 2007, across the world from Ghana to Kenya to Nepal to the Philippines, we began to realize something exciting. We saw children become empowered as readers because we created safe communities for strength building. We started by creating supportive social-emotional frameworks, and the children began to read more rapidly and fearlessly. Local communities played a vital role in turning children into super readers by valuing oral language, home stories, the children's own perspectives, and community-wide celebrations of reading.

 For a video of Pam and Ernest discussing the 7 Strengths Model, visit scholastic.com /superreaderresources.

In addition to providing crucial access to books and technology, LitWorld focuses on investing in children, parents, teachers, families, and community-based organizations to build worlds in which reading is deeply valued. Reading and learning to read became all the more possible because everyone is involved, everyone is a leader. As a literacy empowerment tool, the 7 Strengths Model brings a new dimension to the teaching of reading. LitWorld created a foundation upon which to build a whole world for super readers. In this world, we explicitly value the role of the human spirit in the work of learning to read and the role of the community itself in drawing closer together through reading.

We began to identify our social-emotional framework as seven specific strengths the children were returning to again and again, from country to country and city to city and state to state. These seven strengths were referred to over and over as touchstones for learning, for becoming more powerful as readers. We built safe spaces for reading around the 7 Strengths called "LitClubs," and later, we extended this model to the summer months in "LitCamps," which are now offered across the United States in a partnership between Scholastic and LitWorld to share the model as widely as possible.

Our first LitClub graduates are leaders in their communities. Some are attending college for the first time, others are taking local civic leadership roles. The safe circles of support and the attention to the strength-building social-emotional empowerment skills were the magical ingredients to make reading lives possible. As longtime literacy experts and advocates, we have written this book with the urgent awareness that this model needs to be shared widely because these ideas can create change instantly and dramatically. We are now in more than 60 countries and all across the United States, spreading the work of what it means to be a super reader with thousands of children.

The 7 Strengths are, at the core, egalitarian. They help do away with harmful labels—"struggling," "English language deficit," "at risk," and so on. Even "gifted" separates children from one another and may even limit their understanding of one another as readers. The 7 Strengths Model levels the playing field and at the same time raises expectations for every child.

Children need choice and voice in their work as readers. The 7 Strengths provide a framework for super readers that is based on the ideas that the work of childhood is about formulating reading identities and that academic success is more closely built upon social-emotional, character-rich learning than we might have ever previously thought. 7 Strengths students are actively aware of who they are as readers—their habits, preferences, challenges, and goals—and they understand the importance of each strength in their potential success.

The 7 Strengths Create a Culturally Responsive Reading World

During a global teaching journey to Kisumu, Kenya, that we took, children clamored to see the photos we had taken. But when we turned the screen toward them, they asked us to point out which child they were in the photos. In this community, there were no windows and no mirrors. The children had great difficulty determining their own selves in the images because without the power to make a reflection, they were unable to distinguish themselves from others. The same is true in reading.

For a video of Pam and Ernest discussing implementation of the 7 Strengths Model, visit scholastic.com /superreaderresources.

Rudine Sims Bishop (1990) described the ways in which literature can serve as windows, sliding glass doors, and mirrors. Books can become windows, offering "views of worlds that may be real or imagined, familiar or strange." Readers can then treat these windows as sliding glass doors by walking through them and into the world created by the author. These same windows can also serve as mirrors, reflecting the readers' lives and experiences back to them "as part of the larger human experience." Literature, particularly multicultural literature, can provide both self-affirmation and a way to learn about and appreciate various cultures, dialects, and ways of being in the world. Literature has the power to teach about and honor readers' differences and similarities.

Whether at home with children or in the classroom, let us prioritize the mirrors and windows library, the mirrors and windows world, the mirrors and windows conversations in which every child can find herself and also see out to the larger world.

To introduce their separate op-eds for *The New York Times*, father-son children's book authors Walter Dean Myers and Christopher Myers placed this statement: "Of 3,200 children's books published in 2013, just 93 were about black people, according to a study by the Cooperative Children's Book Center at the University of Wisconsin." This dearth of diversity is tragic for all children, but above all for those who look in books, day after day, never seeing themselves reflected back. Christopher Myers describes how this "apartheid of children's literature" results in children of color who "recognize the boundaries being imposed upon their imaginations, and are certain to imagine themselves well within the borders they are offered, to color themselves inside the lines."

Sherman Alexie, a Native American author, accepted the National Book Award in 2007. He thanked Ezra Jack Keats, author of *The Snowy Day*: "It was the first time I looked at a book and saw a brown, black, beige character—a character who resembled me physically and resembled me spiritually, in all his gorgeous loneliness and splendid isolation."

Every child deserves to know she belongs to the world of reading and the world of writing. Whether white or black, Latino or Asian, boy or girl or transgender—everyone and anyone can, will, and should benefit from a library as diverse as the world we live in. The world is stretching its wings and at long last recognizing that the power of story is central to our human experience. Certainly all children can relate to a good story whether or not the character looks like them. (Think *Goodnight Moon* or *Charlotte's Web*!) But there is no question that we hunger to see ourselves, to have reflections that we can call our own. That a child in the darkest moment finds comfort in a character who "reminds me of me" the way we all do when that pang of recognition makes the journey less lonely.

What Are the 7 Strengths?

The 7 Strengths are habits and feelings that educators and parents must nurture in children to provide them with the foundations they need to become super readers. They are solidly based in the social-emotional research of, among others, Daniel Goleman, an internationally renowned psychologist whose 1995 bestseller *Emotional Intelligence* transformed our understanding of IQ and personal, academic, and workplace success. Lest you think that social-emotional skills like the 7 Strengths are "soft" and can't compete with such cognitively driven skills as problem solving and critical analysis, consider Goleman's 2011 book *Leadership: The Power of Emotional Intelligence*. Goleman notes that some of the best leaders in the corporate world owe their success to their ability to identify and monitor emotions— their own and others'—and to manage relationships. In a similar vein, Mark Edmundson's new book, *Self and Soul: A Defense of Ideals* (2015), asks readers to revisit humanity's "three great ideals: courage, contemplation, and compassion." These are the ideals, Edmundson maintains, that give life both value and meaning. Let us turn now to an exploration of the 7 Strengths that frame our work, how we define them, and language with which you can share them.

 Belonging: *Identifying as a valued, represented member of a larger community*

For a child to flourish, she must know that she is a valued member of a community and that her unique voice is respected. When a child feels as though she doesn't belong, she becomes removed, she disappears from group conversations, she may even act out. Our core sense of belief in ourselves stems from the knowledge that others believe in us, too. Both the classroom and the home can be places for comfort and growth, assuring the child of her value as an individual so that she can go out and affect change in the world.

A child who belongs is known by others. Her reading preferences are known. She knows the reading preferences of others. She is celebrated when she takes a step forward. She celebrates others. Children hunger to belong, to clubs, to groups. Reading is designed to build a social community and super readers are made by building a social community around them.

What you choose to read to children is critical. If a young girl never reads a book with a female main character, how can she take a leading role in her own life? If bilingual children only read books in English, how will they learn that their culture and language are valued? Activities and discussions involving children must reflect their own agency as community members. Our language as teachers must firmly plant children in their identities as powerful readers and writers.

Children thrive as readers when surrounded by reading material and the language of literacy. Books and talk about books help establish a reading or "scholarly" culture in the home, one that persists from generation to generation, largely independent of education and class. This creates a "taste for books" and promotes the skills and knowledge that foster literacy and numeracy and, thus, lead to lifelong academic advantages (Evans et al., 2010).

Kids in this environment embrace books and the reading life. They self-identify as readers who belong to a larger reading community whose members know books, talk about books, share books, and love books.

 ### Curiosity: *Fostering a willingness to explore new territory and test new theories*

Children who ask questions are proactively engaged in their environments and learn to anticipate both problems and solutions. Building a stance of inquiry is crucial for college, career, and civic engagement.

We must create environments that are open and hospitable to the kinds of unique, interesting responses children have to texts and in conversations. Curiosity is a spark that must be fueled by the affirmation of wonderings.

Reading creates curiosity, and books should be seen as a launching pad for further inquiry. Our conversations around texts must expand beyond character analysis to encourage children to look out into the world around them. Project-based learning allows children to follow lines of inquiry of their own choosing, resulting in higher engagement and stronger results. A focus on asking open-ended questions cultivates children's curiosity and fosters an attitude of being "forever learners."

 ### Friendship: *Having close, trusting relationships and personal connections to others—learning to interact in positive, productive ways*

Whether in the home, classroom, or workplace, being able to listen, speak, and connect with others is extremely important. Friendship is a strength that fosters within children a deeper understanding of themselves. Navigating friendships can be difficult, yet it is a powerful and necessary tool that must be cultivated. "Friendship is a highly complex and emotionally demanding transaction and meeting the challenges of friendship requires emotional awareness and applied strengths" (O'Grady, 2012). Psychologists from the University of Illinois and the University of Pennsylvania found that there is a strong correlation between health, happiness, and friendship (Diener & Seligman, 2002).

Being a super reader should not be lonely. We learn better together than by ourselves (Schaps, 2009). Reading is enhanced when we recommend books to one another, when we trust one another, and when we support one another through the hard parts of reading.

Yet, in the traditional classroom that focuses on individual learning, friendship can too often be seen as a distraction, something that can get you into trouble. Because of this, children have not always been explicitly taught how to engage in friendships. Super readers cultivate relationships around the telling and receiving of story. From great literature, they learn about the imperfections of relationships. They empathize with characters and reflect on their own relationships in light of what they have read.

 ## Kindness: *Being compassionate toward others, expressing tenderness that has an impact, near and far*

Kindness is sometimes underrated as something "soft" in our teaching lives. And yet, it is the heartbeat of our civil society and it is what we remember most in both the challenging and joyous times of our lives. In fact, "…scientific studies prove there are many physical, emotional, and mental health benefits associated with kindness" (Currie, 2014). Kindness prevents bullying, it fortifies every single human being, and it powers us forward when we are faced with adversity.

Children can internalize the lessons of kindness from the books they read. They can learn from these stories that being considerate of others goes much further than simply looking out for yourself. Families, librarians, and teachers must make every effort to choose texts that promote ethics and can be used as platforms to hold discussions about social values. A community *without* kindness will not succeed; it is only by working with one another, instead of against, that we can harness the positive energy of our combined agency.

Confidence: *Thinking independently and expressing ideas with assurance*

Confidence is a garden that must be cultivated consistently through the small challenges and triumphs of each day. Whether it's the envy from browsing a friend's seemingly perfect life on social media or frustration from being unable to sound out a difficult word, teachers and caregivers must be there to remind the child that adults struggle with the same issues and that we all have our own strategies to overcome them.

A super reader is able to approach any situation knowing that she has the tools for success within herself. Let us create a genuinely praise-centric and inclusive environment that allows children to feel confident as readers, thinkers, and learners.

Courage: *Having the strength to do something that you know is right, even though it may be difficult*

The struggles children face, whether they're happening at home or at school, are real and require a good dose of courage. Courage can be practiced, and courage can be learned. It is far different from the popular idea of "grit" which sometimes seems to assume that if only a child is tough, that child can overcome obstacles. But courage is not necessarily about toughness. Courage is more about tapping into one's capacity to do the right thing even when it feels difficult. One may need courage to show kindness. One may need courage to warmly welcome an outsider. One may need courage to stay silent or pay a compliment instead of criticizing.

By practicing courage and teaching it, we can help children become more courageous readers—readers who push through the hard parts and face reading challenges fearlessly. Children can learn from the difficulties and victories of the characters they encounter in literature. As readers, they can celebrate their triumphs and mourn their losses. Families, teachers, and librarians can help children apply those lessons from literature to their own lives, showing them that if they have the courage to take risks, to make themselves vulnerable, it will pay off in positive results. To facilitate this learning, children need access to books that reflect the complex nature of courage, which often has little to do with success or failure and everything to do with trying your best and persevering when faced with adversity. These types of stories are chock full of teachable moments that can be expanded into larger discussions around our multifaceted understanding of courage.

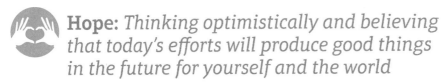 **Hope:** *Thinking optimistically and believing that today's efforts will produce good things in the future for yourself and the world*

Perhaps the most important quality that a child can possess is hope. A child who has hope believes in herself and her capacity to make good things happen in her life. She is ready to recognize the advantages that literacy brings. She will be willing to pursue the knowledge and engage in activities that help her grow as a reader and writer. She is able to envision a future where she is secure and successful. A wise teacher realizes that before building skills and teaching strategies, he must help a child find reasons to be hopeful.

Literature has the power to give wings to our dreams, introducing us to possibilities for the future, reinterpretations of the past, and alternates to the present. Through exposure to books, children are able to read about a female president of the United States, or they can imagine living on Mars or having superpowers. They can travel to the edge of the galaxy or the top of Mount Everest, they can swim with dolphins or multiply with microbes. Transformational stories allow super readers the empowerment of a flexible frame of mind, one that can grow with their dreams. And super readers are big dreamers—they are eager to play their role in making the impossible possible.

The 7 Strengths

BELONGING: Identifying as a valued, represented member of a larger community

CURIOSITY: Fostering a willingness to explore new territory and test new theories

FRIENDSHIP: Having close, trusting relationships and personal connections to others—learning to interact in positive, productive ways

KINDNESS: Being compassionate toward others, expressing tenderness that has an impact, near and far

CONFIDENCE: Thinking independently and expressing ideas with assurance

COURAGE: Having the strength to do something that you know is right, even though it may be difficult

HOPE: Thinking optimistically and believing that today's efforts will produce good things in the future for yourself and the world

Family Guide

Top 10 Ways to Nurture a Super Reader

1 Value your child and his or her stories.

You can make your child's reading future brighter by making it clear that his or her stories matter to the life of the classroom, home, and community.

The 7 Strengths help children access their stories through connections to texts they read or that are read aloud to them and in conversations with you. We invite you to use these questions to prompt those conversations:

Strength	Questions to Elicit Stories From Your Child
BELONGING	• When have you felt you were part of a group or community? • What kind of communities have you read about lately?
CURIOSITY	• What questions do you have? • What are you wondering about in something you are reading or have read lately?
FRIENDSHIP	• When have you felt a connection to another person? • When has a friendship from a book inspired you?
KINDNESS	• When have you reached out to others? • What books are you reading (or are we reading) that show kindness?
CONFIDENCE	• When have you felt bold? • Have you ever read something that made you feel more confident?
COURAGE	• What makes you feel brave? • What stories have you read that inspired you to be courageous?
HOPE	• What are your dreams? • What new ideas, hopes, and dreams has your reading inspired?

2 Invite your child into a safe and supportive reading environment.

As part of a family, you provide the security and support your child needs to take risks to grow as a reader. Let your child know you value his or her development as a reader by creating:

- cozy physical spaces as havens for reading and rereading favorite books
- a quiet corner where he or she can always find solitude
- baskets where he or she can keep favorite books

Value reading of all kinds—even reading we don't always consider "serious," such as the backs of cereal boxes and comic books. Make sure your child knows it's okay to read easier books, and to reread them, because it's something super readers do all the time, plus it builds stamina and confidence.

The language you use to invite your child to join you in a reading environment will make a lifelong impact. Use comments like:

- I value you as a reader.
- Let's read together. I love to read with you!
- I sometimes struggle as a reader, too, and want you to know that it is totally normal.
- I see you rereading favorite books. That is a great thing for a super reader to do!
- Tell me what would make our home more comfortable for you as a reader.

3 Dedicate daily time for your child to read for pleasure.

The more children are encouraged to read for pleasure, the more likely they are to become engaged readers (Guthrie, 2004) and develop identities as readers. In *You Gotta BE the Book: Teaching Engaged and Reflective Reading With Adolescents*, Jeffrey Wilhelm (1996) advocates for middle school students to have freedom to read "fun" books in class. When he allowed students to choose books themselves, he found they became more excited about reading and read more. Donalyn Miller (2009) found that when she provided time for her sixth graders to read the books they picked themselves, they read 40 to 50 books a year—far more than they had read in previous years.

Create uninterrupted time every day for pleasure reading at home, even if it's only ten minutes. If necessary, set a timer and say something like, "Let's read together for six minutes tonight!" to show your child you read for pleasure, too. And don't limit yourselves in terms of what you read—from the sports section to the comics to a recipe, read what you like to read. If you don't like to read, or you struggle to read, admit that to your child and say: "Let's work on liking it more together!"

4 Read aloud, read aloud, read aloud.

Reading aloud to children is a research-proven strategy for helping them learn to read, which may seem counterintuitive. After all, if the child is not doing the reading herself, how can she become better at it? Because she is marinating in language. She is swimming in a delightful bath of words. Reading aloud also inspires children to pick up books on their own and exposes them to lots of new vocabulary and a range of texts they may not be able to read on their own. In short, reading aloud inspires them to become super readers.

Make time for reading aloud each day. Make it a ritual. If you are all tired in the evening, read aloud in the morning. Or have your child read aloud to you while you are preparing dinner. Read aloud during bath time. Think waterproof books! Read aloud while waiting on line at the store. Have a book with you to read aloud wherever you go. Tuck it in.

5 Honor your child's own varied reading choices.

If our goal is to develop lifelong readers, let us not judge their quirky, funny, eccentric choices. Children will learn how powerfully books can speak to them, entertain them, instruct them, and help to build their identities as super readers if they are allowed make their own choices and are made to feel good about those choices. Make sure your child gets that chance.

6 Provide daily access to books and stories in all forms, genres, and platforms.

It has been said of dancers, athletes, musicians, and other experts that just a day away from their practice makes them rusty. The same can be said of readers. Let your children read anything and everything every day! In that way, their stamina grows, and they become prepared for any challenge reading may bring. Encourage your child to read online, offline, short texts, long ones, serious ones, funny ones, fiction, and nonfiction. All texts are, in so many ways, helping your child become a super reader.

7 Champion rereading.

Each time a super reader rereads a book, it is a new experience because he is constantly growing and changing as a reader. Although the words on the page do not change, the reader does because his interpretations change each time he revisits a favorite book. Encourage your child to reread, letting him or her know that rereading builds stamina, deepens comprehension, and enhances knowledge. If your child is rereading voluntarily, do not assume it is because he or she wants reading to feel "easy." Rereading takes work. Just as we may prepare a favorite dish again and again to become a better cook , so too a child may read a favorite book again and again to become a better reader.

8 Help your child see authors as real people making real decisions.
Invite your child to look at examples of author's notes, forewords, acknowledgment pages, and endnotes in books, as well as author websites and blogs. By doing that, he or she will see authors as real people.

Encourage your child to reach out to authors personally. In this era of social media, authors are far more accessible than ever before, and even a brief reply is thrilling for your child—and will fuel his or her desire to read and write.

9 Value your child's talk and exchanges of ideas.
Talking about what we've read is an important part of being in a community of readers. Whether they're at the dinner table or in front of classmates, children need space to share their ideas and hear the ideas of others. Why? First and foremost, it shows children that their words are valuable. It also allows children to process how they are learning. As they share ideas, they develop and refine those ideas. Reading is essential, but reading and talking is where all the magic happens—the greatest learning. Ask open-ended questions such as, "What did you think?" rather than statements about what *you* think. Also, encourage your child to express his or her opinions about books because that is a sign of a super reader.

10 Be a reading role model.
We have a wonderful opportunity to model super reading for children. Children should see us reading to learn and reading for pleasure. Whether we are reading a book, the morning paper, a recipe, or a website on some topic that interests us, children should see us reading! And it is okay if they see us struggle. We read above our "level," below our "level," and right at our "level." We read "uphill" books and "downhill" books. We read jokes from a friend and subway maps. In this age of tablets and smartphones, it is harder to be conspicuous reading role models for children. They often can't detect if we are actually reading—or just playing a game. For that reason, make sure to share what you're doing with your child. ("I love this funny article I am reading." or "I got this message from my boss that was hard to understand, so I'm rereading it.") The key here: Be yourself. Your child loves you and admires you. He or she will see you care about reading and will likely care just as much.

Next Steps in the Journey

Together, the 7 Strengths provide a framework for valuing the child, for welcoming her into a community of readers, and for developing her desire and skill to speak and act in the world. In Chapters 3 to 9, we look at each strength up close. We speak to why each strength matters, what it looks like in practice, how to use a favorite children's book to deepen children's understanding of the strength, and how to help families support the strength at home.

CHAPTER 3

STRENGTH 1: BELONGING

"It is really hard to be lonely very long in a world of words. Even if you don't have friends somewhere, you still have language, and it will find you and wrap its little syllables around you and suddenly there will be a story to live in."

—NAOMI SHIHAB NYE

Jaslyn was facing a new school year. The first day of third grade was coming soon. Her mother helped her pick out her first-day outfit and purchase a new purple lunch box. She was ready. When the day came for the publishing of the class lists, she bounced eagerly into the car. "Who do you hope you see on that list, Jaslyn?" her mother asked. Jaslyn's response was quick. "Ariana—and Dominic and Ella! I crossed my fingers and toes and wished last night that we are in class together," she said. "Why?" inquired her mom. "It's so much better when you know your friends are going to be with you. It's a safe feeling. Plus, we like to work together. We trade books when we like one and we like to read each other's stories. Being with them makes me feel happy."

 For a video snapshot of belonging in action, visit scholastic.com /superreaderresources.

When Jorge started his after-school program, he was learning English for the first time. He was eight years old. He was from Guyana, and he was also hearing impaired. His after-school leader invited him to share what he loved to do back at home and he said that he was a good caretaker of animals. She invited him to create a basket of animal books with her and to become the "animal book expert" for his classmates. That helped Jorge feel a sense of belonging with his classmates, who soon crossed all language barriers to find out the latest animal he was reading about.

Belonging to a group is as basic a human need as nourishment and shelter. We are wired to need each other, and it fuels our learning to be in a safe, supportive belonging community. Children thrive when they belong, when they feel safe and surrounded by a community that values their presence. What better opportunity to provide this healthy sense of belonging than in a classroom? When the classroom stakeholders—students, teachers, school staff members, and families—come together, that kind of community is bound to flourish.

What does this have to do with reading? First, belonging to a community and feeling safe, positive, and happy in it helps children become empowered and more connected to the work that is required within the class. They'll be eager to do the reading work because they feel valued. Secondly, when the community identifies itself by its very nature as a group of avid readers and hard-working authors, the child's identity becomes tied to that definition. "I am a member of this mighty group that so values super reading and writing, so therefore, I too am a super reader!"

Why Belonging Matters

There is strong evidence that having human connections and being successful at school are related. We have decades of research that suggests having at least one strong and stable relationship with a supportive adult is a key factor in helping children cope with high-stress situations (Harvard University's Center on the Developing Child, 2015). While that relationship is ideally found in the home, it can be found elsewhere, such as school. The teacher-student relationship is an ideal support for those students who may lack a sense of belonging in the home, and it can also give children who do enjoy a rich family life an even stronger sense of belonging, particularly when families and teachers work together.

Relationships matter a great deal in the 7 Strengths classroom. The teacher serves as coach and guide, nurturing the child's assets.

Much of the research that supports belonging can be traced back to the work of John Bowlby, a British psychologist, who studied the negative impact on children's social and emotional development, with the loss of or significant absence of a parent or primary caregiver (Bowlby, 1969). Bowlby's ideas on attachment and belonging have been taken seriously by educational researchers. In Bergin and Bergin's review of attachment research in education (2009), they argue that secure attachments to teachers, administrators, and other students are the foundation of children's social and emotional well-being in school. Students who develop meaningful attachments to teachers and classmates also develop meaningful attachments to the work of the classroom. Those attachments provide the foundation to identify as an engaged and capable reader, which is so crucial to reading success. Super readers need to belong to a community of super readers.

What You Can Do to Promote Belonging in School and in Out-of-School Programs

Make heart maps.

The great writer and educator, poet, and leader Georgia Heard has shared with us her beautiful heart maps (2016). Heart maps have become a signature way for us at LitWorld to build a sense of belonging in children as readers and learners, all across the year. A heart map is a graphic representation of things that students hold dear in their hearts. Make the shape of a heart out of paper large enough for students to fill it up with writing (or online in their tablets). Have students divide their hearts as they wish and write things that are "in their heart"—people, pets, books, and ideas that are dear to them—in those sections. They can write about and also look for books about the things they included on their heart maps. You can use heart maps in many ways to get conversations going in the classroom (and at home). For example, you can invite the children to create heart maps of:

- longings in their hearts
- people who have influenced them

- places that have touched them
- their hopes and dreams
- their wonderings

By sketching heart maps, children can use them as conversation starters with others, find a place of belonging in the classroom, and make space for others' ideas, too.

Create digital spaces for students and families.

Creating digital spaces for students and families promotes collaboration and a sense of belonging. Children can post in a discussion forum such as voicethread.com to share writing about reading or respond to longer conversations about a favorite text or group of texts. Creating a sense of belonging through the virtual community helps families join in, too, to see what children are working on and to watch the reading identity grow and blossom in each child. Some possible prompts to encourage the spirit of belonging may include:

- How do you feel you are growing as a reader this week?
- What titles or types of books can you recommend to friends?
- What kinds of affirmations can you share with your reading friends?

Personalize the classroom library.

The crown jewel in a community of super readers is the classroom library, both on- and offline. The collection owned and cared for by the community should reflect the work and preferences of members of that community, which means that your classroom library will change every year and also throughout the year. The classroom library should be referred to as "ours," and the care and curating of it should be the responsibility of everyone who uses it. Make sure all students are familiar with the various sections of their library. Create a sense of ownership by inviting students to add books from home to the collection, and request specific additions they know they like. Decide on key points in the year when children can create new baskets or files, and create new categories (for example, stories with courageous characters and Mo Willem books). Create a place where students can make recommendations to friends near the bins or online.

Value, promote, and actively advocate for powerful diversity in the classroom library. Every student should be able to see his own self or hear a voice that speaks her language in the pages of books as well as have the opportunity to hear from many voices and perspectives. Children should see the library as a window to the world. Display and honor books, stories, and information that reflects the lives of people around the globe, people of all nationalities, cultures, ethnic groups, gender perspectives, and linguistic backgrounds. In a "belonging" library, children can say, "I see myself in this collection" and "I see a world I want to know about." (See page 150 for more information on the classroom library.)

Design an environment that supports belonging.

Make the wall space come alive with children's work. The wall space to create a world of belonging for children can include a bulletin board called "Welcome to My World," where each child gets to imagine/wonder/remember/observe the kind of world she wants us to know is hers. She can bring images, photos, art, and found objects from her life at home and school to post on that board. This can also be done virtually if you have access to Internet tools that other children can visit and browse.

We can also build our belonging communities through read aloud. Books such as *The Recess Queen, Wonder, My People, Weslandia, Sitti's Secrets,* and Walt Whitman's *Leaves of Grass* all point out the important theme of belonging. *The Recess Queen* is specifically about the child who recognizes her need to be part of a community of her peers; *My People* speaks eloquently through the poetry of Langston Hughes about what it means to fight a fierce battle for belonging; *Weslandia* is an enchanted look at another universe where one can belong in new ways; *Sitti's Secrets* is about how belonging can reach across oceans; and *Leaves of Grass* points to the radical voice that Whitman shared in the 1800s that spoke to democracy and the ultimate notion that belonging is for everyone. Each of those texts relates directly to the concept of belonging and can help students construct their own ideas about belonging to their family, community, school, and wider world. By affirming the growth of the child every day, week, and month, we are saying: "Yes, you belong here as a reader." Examples of what we mean by that include:

- I admire how you've been spending more time reading these days.

- I notice that you are the kind of reader who likes to read with a partner.

- It was so exciting to see you take a new step as a reader today.

- I observed that you like to reread familiar text, and that is something great readers do.

To create a sense of belonging for all readers, reading time should include plenty of opportunities for students to talk with one another. Ask the following questions—and post them for students to ask one another:

- What book did you fall in love with this week?

- What kind of reading most lights your fire?

- Where did reading feel hard, and how can we be of help?

Belonging classrooms encourage and support a lot of talk, and that talk is trusting and safe. Readers can jump-start and facilitate conversation; they can help other readers go deeper in conversation. Peer conversations in partnerships, small groups, and whole-class scenarios support the kind of deeper thinking and analysis needed for super reading. In belonging classrooms, students consult with one another to choose reading materials. They invite each other to work through the hard parts of texts together and sit and do the work of close readers when texts push them beyond their levels of understanding. They use language like the following:

- I am enthusiastic about what you said about…

- I learned _____ from you as a reader today.

- I want to add on to what you said about that passage.

- I hear you, but I have another point of view to contribute.

- I love that book, too!

- I have a different opinion, and I want to deepen our conversation by sharing it.

Community River Maps

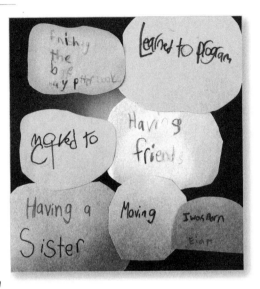

By incorporating information about your reading community on a Community River Map, you can foster a sense of belonging and recognize what connects super readers and what makes each one of them unique.

Directions

1. Introduce the lesson by saying:

   Readers become stronger when they belong to a strong reading community. Today's lesson will help us learn more about each other. This will help us grow closer as a group and see ways that we can support each other as readers.

   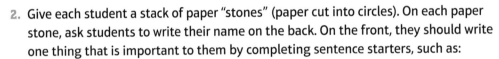

2. Give each student a stack of paper "stones" (paper cut into circles). On each paper stone, ask students to write their name on the back. On the front, they should write one thing that is important to them by completing sentence starters, such as:

   - *I like to learn about…*
   - *My favorite author is…*
   - *My favorite genre (type of book) is…*
   - *Something that makes me happy is…*
   - *When I read, I like to…*
   - *Something I like to do for fun is…*
   - *I can help classmates with…*

3. Create a "river" for students to place their stones. (This can be a long piece of paper taped on the wall.) Once students have created their stones, they can affix them to the river with tape. Depending on the length of your "river," you may want to limit the number of "stones" each student contributes. You also may want them to create a list of possibilities on a piece of paper first before they write on their stones.

4. Once students have incorporated all of their stones, have them peruse the river and look at the contributions of their classmates. Emphasize things that many students share. To spark conversation, you can ask:

- *Looking at our Community River Map, what do you notice that a lot of us have in common?*

- *Are there more similarities or differences?*

- *How does discovering things we share in common help us as a reading community?*

- *How does discovering what makes us unique help us as a reading community?*

- *What prompts did a lot of us choose? Why do you think so?*

- *What prompts were less common? Why do you think so?*

- *How can all of these discoveries help us grow and strengthen our reading community?*

5. Keep the Community River Map up for a few days as is. Then take down the stones and distribute them to the owners. On a large piece of paper with their names showing, have students draw a picture of themselves and glue the stones to the poster. Invite them to add more stones if they wish. Hang the poster so students can learn about each other as individuals to support their work together as readers. Encourage students to connect with each other. For example, they might use this information to share books that might interest other group members, work together in interest groups, and go to "experts" in the class on various topics.

Actions for Promoting Belonging in School and in Out-of-School Programs

Book Baskets	Create personalized book baskets for each student to curate his or her own reading collection.
Heart Maps	Have each student draw a heart on a sheet of paper, and then fill it with words and images that represent places where and times when he or she has felt a deep sense of belonging.
Belonging Bulletin	Create a personalized corner of a bulletin board in the classroom for each child in the class to share about his or her passions.
Welcome to My World	Students can use their imagination or things they've observed to not only think about the world now, but to mention positive things they would like to add to or change about the world today. They can then conceptualize this world on a poster board and share as a group.
Hand Circle	Create a hand circle using a large poster board. First, all students will place one of their hands around the paper to form a circle. Then, students will trace the outline of their hands. Within the circle that is formed by all of their hands, students will write down things they want to keep in the class. The teacher may offer ideas like joy, fun, and smiles. On the space outside of the circle of hands, students will write down things they want to leave out of their classroom community, like hurtful comments and negativity.

CLOSE READING LESSON

My Brother Charlie

BY HOLLY ROBINSON PEETE AND RYAN ELIZABETH PEETE
ILLUSTRATED BY SHANE EVANS

Close reading is a thorough reading and rereading of text, making the process of reading visible. We demonstrate the reading process, illuminate fine writing techniques, and connect themes in support of the 7 Strengths Model.

Summary: *My Brother Charlie* is the story of a little girl named Callie and her twin brother, Charlie, who has autism. Throughout the story, Callie explains how Charlie is a valued member of her family, and what Charlie contributes.

BEFORE READING

Discuss Belonging:
- What groups or places give you a sense of belonging?
- How might belonging somewhere help you? What kinds of actions do others take that make you feel you belong?

Discuss the Book's Cover:
- What might the two siblings be feeling about their relationship?
- To what group might the little girl and her brother both belong?

DURING READING

Interpretation:
- How might Callie feel? How do you know? What evidence do you find in the text?
- Do you think Charlie feels a sense of belonging in his family?

When Charlie wants something, nothing stops him. Even when it's dangerous. And there are days when it's hard to be Charlie's sister. Sometimes he can ruin the best playdates. Other times he seems so far away, like when he won't look at me. Or speak. Or play.

Author's Craft:
How do the authors' sentences and illustrator's drawings show Callie's emotions?

Charlie has autism. But autism doesn't have Charlie. If you ever get to meet my brother, you'll feel lucky to be his friend. He won't care if you have the coolest sneakers, or if you are the best at sports. He'll just like you for who you really are. That's Charlie.

I'm blessed to be Charlie's sister and to share so much. I count my "Charlie Blessings" every day. At the very top of my "Charlie Blessings" list is the love Charlie and I have for each other.

Interpretation:
What opinion does the author have about why Charlie is an important part of the family?
What might Callie say to someone who asks about her family?

AFTER READING

What groups or communities do you belong to? How does belonging to them make a difference in your life?
How can we make a commitment to each other to be sure we all belong to our learning community?

▶ **For other favorite books on belonging, see page 198.**

For other favorite books on belonging, see page 198.

iMovie: Have students work together to create end-of-unit slide shows and short films that celebrate reading, using books on the belonging list, or create films that represent belonging to a club, a family, or the natural world.

Twitter account: Create a class or family Twitter account. Have students work together to create hashtag campaigns that promote belonging themes that are connected to the books you read.

Kidblog: Share favorite belonging books online.

Online book reviews: Gather ideas for new books to read that will cultivate a discussion around belonging (e.g., anti-bullying, groups students belong to).

Google Doc: Create a class Google Doc for students to share their ideas, reflections, and comments about the books they are reading and the books you are reading to them.

What You Can Do to Promote Belonging at Home

Debbie Lera, master teacher, reports:

I recently looped with my class from second to third grade. I knew the research supported looping in terms of building a strong community, so I jumped at the opportunity to try it.

I'm now in the second week of year two, and the benefits have been abundant and even surprising. The families already like and support one another and their children. They trust and like me, and we have this village feeling where we are all wrapped around this group of children. I feel so much more comfortable in my second year than I ever allowed myself to feel with a new group.

I hosted a conversation with the families where everyone had wonderful opinions about what books their kids like to read, and they learned from each other, grabbed sticky notes, and wrote down titles. We decided to have book gatherings where the families come in once a month to share their book preferences. We talked about our local bookstore (some had been there, others hadn't), and I heard conversations like, "Just go in and talk to Cinda. She's amazing and can match books to your boys easily. Just tell her what they like and she'll pull out five titles."

Together, we made plans for a take-one leave-one book basket in the classroom, and a book blog where they can share the titles their children liked. We made plans and committed to three family reads for every family this year.

Although I had the benefit of a second year with the same group, I saw that this type of community building would have been possible within a single year as well. Why did I talk the entire time during Back-to-School Night in prior years? Why hadn't I been more interactive? Why hadn't I asked the opinions of the families until that second year? What magic would have happened if I had invited the families to gather regularly?

We can help mothers, fathers, grandparents, older siblings, and caregivers to feel a sense of belonging to reading that we do in school and also help them embrace the child into a community of readers at home. We can support families in how best to ask children to describe the day's work and listen and give practical tips for all families to encourage children to explore their emerging reader identities.

By sharing the family guides at the end of this chapter and the following six chapters, along with the appendix of children's books organized according to the 7 Strengths, families can cultivate what Donalyn Miller calls book whispering talents (Miller, 2009), making great recommendations to their children to get them motivated. Let's encourage families to think of reading as a "together" activity to foster that sense of belonging. Adults and children can read different texts side by side, read multiple copies of the same book independently, or share a book. We recognize that not all adults in families will feel comfortable reading aloud if their own reading skills do not feel strong. We can support all families by encouraging reading aloud through pictures in picture books, or by sending home specific questions that can help lead to discussion of the pictures and the big themes in texts children are reading so that all families can enjoy books together, no matter their reading skills. (Find the family guides and appendix at scholastic.com /superreaderresources.)

We often praise children who are star athletes. We line courts and fields each weekend, encouraging them. There's no mistaking whose kid just scored a goal, you only need to listen for the loudest, proudest voices! And those children are also beaming, not only because of their individual successes, but in seeing how proud and happy they have made their families. Imagine what it would do for children's reading identities if they were honored and praised for their reading in the same way. Create spaces for students to share their writing so that their families can celebrate the effort just as they would a virtuoso piano performance or a game-winning three-point shot.

Super Reader Family Guide

Actions to Develop Your Child's Sense of Belonging

Book Baskets

Create personalized book baskets for each family member that reflect the passions and interests of each person, honoring every member as a cherished member of this family unit.

Heart Maps

Have each family member draw a heart on a sheet of paper or on the computer and then fill it with words and images that represent where he or she has felt a deep sense of belonging.

Belonging Bulletin

Create a bulletin board in your home for each family member to feature his or her passions.

Family Interviews

Have your child interview family members about groups and communities to which they belong. They can ask questions like:

- Who is your best friend and why?
- What is your favorite thing to do?
- What was your favorite thing to do when you were my age?
- What group has felt important to you in your life?
- Where did you feel the greatest sense of belonging as a child?

Family Mural

Create a mural together with images that represent each member of the family.

Family Favorites Book

As a family, compile a list of your favorite things to do together. Talk about your favorite things using questions including:

- What is your favorite book to read aloud?
- What is your favorite song to dance to together?
- Decorate your book with images and mementos, and keep it in a place of honor!

Routines to Develop Your Child's Sense of Belonging

- Create read aloud times that are rituals, and make sure every member gets a chance to select the reading.

- Talk about favorite and current reading material, from cereal boxes to novels.

- Choose books to read as a whole family.

- Create a listening corner for books online or on tape so multigenerations can listen together.

- Create book baskets or online files labeled with your child's name and add to those baskets/files whenever your child develops new interests (soccer, for example, and then add soccer books)

- Notice and celebrate unique qualities of your child as a reader. (Sarah loves animal books. Carlos reads books aloud to his little brother.)

- Share your child's reading growth with grandparents.

- Encourage siblings to read together.

- Have your child read to a pet or a stuffed animal!

- Host reading celebrations at home (tea and cake, etc.).

- Affirm and praise small steps in your child's reading progress.

- Post reading accomplishments on the refrigerator or wall for all to see.

CHAPTER 4

STRENGTH 2: CURIOSITY

"Curiosity is more important than knowledge."
—ALBERT EINSTEIN

After reading the entire seven-book Harry Potter series by J. K. Rowling, Antonio, a 10-year-old, announces that he is going to invent his own sport in honor of Rowling's Quidditch game. Encouraged by his parents and his older sibling, he sets out on his task. First, he must develop a name and a concept for his sport, and then, he must develop rules. In order to understand how his sport will be governed, Antonio begins to perform Google searches of other sports. On his own free time he is analyzing the dimensions of playing fields and visiting the websites of other sports associations to gain a better understanding of the genre. He even finds that a few college campuses in the U.S. now field Quidditch teams! Once he is on his way, Antonio creates a Google document that he shares with his family so that they can keep track of his progress. "What should I do once I am finished with the sport?" he asks. I don't know, maybe pitch it to the Olympic committee!

In Los Angeles, a group of early adolescents are reading Rudolfo Anaya's *Bless Me, Ultima,* a novel that features a 12-year-old protagonist who is caught between the worlds of Mexico and the United States. As many of the students in the class are also recent immigrants from Mexico, they become interested in their own families' stories of immigration. The final project for the unit involves students conducting oral history interviews with two elders in their family. The students create short reports about these interviews that are accompanied by slide show presentations that they share with their classmates, family, and friends. Many of the students and their families comment that they learned things about themselves and

 For a video snapshot of curiosity in action, visit scholastic.com/superreaderresources.

their families that they would not have known were it not for the oral history assignment. The curiosity sparked by reading a story opened the opportunity for early adolescents to conduct their own research in their families and communities.

Young Fiona, age 6, is curious about nursing homes. Her grandpa, who has lived with the family since she was born, is now moving to one. In the 7 Strengths classroom, she is encouraged to explore her curious questions, interview her grandfather and his friends, read and reread their responses, and write a "research" report on her perspective. She determined that "Nursing homes are pretty good because Grandad and his friends like the Macaroni and Cheese Fridays!"

Why Curiosity Matters

Curiosity leads to invention and innovation. Bill Gates, Steve Jobs, Indra Nooyi, and other creative CEOs have prized curiosity in the workplace because it helps colleagues solve problems and work collaboratively (Gates, 2000). It is a strength that reaches across disciplines and is seen in the youngest child—the child who explores the world by asking "Why? Why? Why?"

Children are naturally hungry for information. Babies explore by touching and tasting, gazing with wide-eyed wonder at the world around them. As they get older, children question, which is a reflection of an ingrained need to always know more.

That curiosity, though, which is often so evident in a child's early life, is often suppressed in a school that values quiet obedience over active learning. In Susan Engel's classroom study, curiosity was measured by the

number of questions asked in a two-hour period (Engel, 2015). While kindergartners asked 2 to 5 questions in this time frame, many fifth graders went a full day without showing any signs of inquisitiveness. The lack of questions in classrooms is a direct consequence of children's disengagement from reading, writing, and a love of learning. Without this critical engagement, we deprive children of their most powerful tool for achievement: their own insatiable appetites for knowledge.

Curiosity leads super readers to unknown territory, and they can't chart a new course without circling back a few times. They will not be able to be curious if they see failure as a negative. A recently published article in the *Harvard Business Review* contends that, in today's complex world, curiosity is as important as intelligence. (*Harvard Business Review*, 2014)

What You Can Do to Promote Curiosity in School and in Out-of-School Programs

Practice KWL.

Curiosity in the classroom blossoms when the community to which all students belong is healthy and supportive. There are many ways to encourage curiosity. The classroom is the ideal space to teach students to ask questions, to wonder, and to celebrate those behaviors when you spot them. In our classrooms, students should be encouraged to ask questions

of text, of the world, and of each other. A popular strategy for introducing a new topic is a KWL. A KWL is used at the beginning of a unit to establish what students already "Know" about a topic and what they "Want to know." Their responses are revisited at the end of the unit as way for students to reflect on what they have "Learned." KWL encourages students to ask questions about a topic and monitor their background knowledge. You might decide to have students complete a KWL graphic organizer or incorporate technology. On an interactive whiteboard, you can record and categorize student responses as they complete a KWL chart together.

Embrace inquiry-based instruction.

You can have students actively involved in following a line of inquiry inspired by the books that they are reading. Identify driving questions for inquiry and share those questions with the students. (For example, a teacher asks the class, "What makes a person a hero?" and shares that she herself is not sure about the answer, and invites students to join her as they together uncover an answer.) Also, questions can be geared toward identifying a problem that needs solving, thereby launching a research and/or engineering cycle. ("Why do so many kids not finish their school lunch?" "What can we build that will keep the deer away from our garden so our plants can thrive?")

Use literature to foster wonderings.

Through the read aloud and close reading experiences, children can come to see literature as a springboard for their own deepest questions and wonderings. They can use literature as a launching point for independent research, or for turn-and-talk discussions with a partner. (See Chapter 10 for more information.) In modeling curiosity, ask open-ended questions that lead to lines of inquiry for you and your students.

Some of the prompts we can use to encourage engagement and curiosity around text include:

- Stop and jot a wondering you have right now about what you are reading.

- Why are you feeling moved by this text?

- Why do you think the author made that decision?

- What is your opinion/claim/hypothesis about (a character, plot, setting, idea, fact)?

- What are you curious to learn more about?

With a true "mirrors and windows" text collection, super readers will have natural wonderings about the world of diverse peoples and cultures, languages, and customs. (See Chapter 10 for more information.) They will wonder about their own lives in the context of their homes and their families, communities, and world.

- What are you wondering about your own culture and language?

- How can you ask your family or community questions that would guide you to more knowledge?

- What are you wondering about other people who live in different places?

- How can we find out more about our wonderings?

In this era of higher standards, there is a renewed appreciation for the use of primary source documents in the classroom. In studying American history, one fifth-grade class read drafts of the Gettysburg Address and also read the speech given by Senator Edward Everett for two hours before Lincoln spoke, comparing the two and discussing why Lincoln's was the forever remembered one (beside the obvious point that his was two minutes long rather than two hours!). In a first-grade class, the children read the notes written by author Nic Bishop about how he uses primary sources as a way to drive and deepen his curiosity for the world. He writes: "I love to play science detective and dig my way down to the bedrock of scientific data published in the primary literature. As well as really being able to check up on the facts, written in the scientist's own words, I can sometimes find new things to use in my books." He revels in the joy of "sifting through the scientist's original tables and charts."

Use the world as a lens to build curiosity.

Affirm children's desire to marvel at ideas, whether they are gathered around a book, looking out the window, or being outdoors together. If you see them wondering about something in nature, in a book they are reading or outside, capture their curiosity by making book baskets (or bookmarks online) for their big topics of wondering. Have easily available informational texts, scientific journals, magazines, and picture books that reflect the passions of the children, from sports to collections to popular culture. More value is placed on the questions students ask than on students finding correct answers to teacher-created questions. Let us create safe environments in which to ask questions that we and the children don't know the answers to. Let us post our favorite wonderings and keep them up on the walls with boxes of index cards nearby so children can add on to their thinking as the year progresses, to bigger questions that take longer to answer. ("How long would it take for a turtle to cross the United States?" "What kinds of family stories do the Navajo Tribe tell?" "Who invented Disney movies and how did they get made?")

Value the power of peer-to-peer interaction.

In the 7 Strengths classroom, student-to-student interaction should be valued in terms of the asking of questions—asking each other questions and sharing longer-term wonderings, as well as making plans for how to do research together to get wonderings answered.

How do students use literature? When someone reads *To Kill a Mockingbird*—or *Native Son* or *Beloved*—part of the spirit of those books is to think about how it makes you think about society. Kids become digital archivists. What was life like in this time? Our students can find deeper ways to explore these questions if they have time each day for informal talk about text.

Model great questioning by turning surface level questions—"What is the author teaching us about?"—into questions that uncover a deeper meaning: "Why did the author choose these text features to convey meaning?" Post exemplar questions for discussing literary texts ("What might the illustration tell you about the character's feelings?" "What may be making the character change her mind?" "What lesson could we learn from what happened in the story?") as well as informational texts ("Does the author appear to be objective or biased? Why?" "What words or phrases did the author use to try to persuade you?" "What do you think the author needed to do to prepare to write this piece?"). Encourage super readers to consider point of view: "What aspects of the text reveal the author's point of view or purpose?" "Why is it important to identify the points of view of others and how they are alike or differ from our own?"

CURIOSITY FOCUS LESSON

Curiosity Poems

By incorporating super readers' questions about the world in poems, you can encourage them to think deeply about topics that make them curious and spark their desire to read to find out more.

Directions

1. **Introduce the lesson by saying:**

   Think about the world around you. Do you ever find yourself asking questions, such as "Why is the sky blue?" or "Why is the grass green?" or "What if I had been born in a different country?" Those kinds of questions keep us wondering and learning all the time. Today we are going to take our questions and turn them into poems, and then turn them into art!

2. **Ask students to think about questions they might have about their world. You can say:**

   Think about your world. What is one thing you are interested in? If you could ask one question about that thing, what would it be? Take a moment and try to pick one question that really gets you thinking!

3. **Invite each student to write a poem based on his or her question. You can say:**

   Now we are going to turn our questions into poems! You can write any type of poem you like, rhyming or no rhyme, short or long! Any type of poem you come up with is great, as long as it asks a question about the thing you are interested in.

   If a student struggles to write a poem, suggest that he or she use the question as the first line of the poem, or as the title.

4. **Have students decorate their work any way they choose. Depending on what materials you have, they may create drawings, cut and glue images, and do anything else to make their poems even more exciting.**

5. **Once students have finished writing and decorating, have them share the poems with others. Depending on the size of your class and the amount of time you have, you may invite people to come up and share with everyone, or do a "turn and talk" with a partner.**

6. Lead a discussion about the activity with students. Ask them questions such as:

- How did it feel to write a poem about a topic you are curious about? Was it hard or easy? Why?

- Did writing this poem spark any more questions for you about your topic?

- Did you learn anything about one of your classmates or the topic of the poem after listening to his or her poem?

- How can you find out more about your topic? (Encourage students to be specific. e.g., "a website about pandas" vs. "the Internet.")

7. Display students' poetry proudly! You can have a "Question Wall" where you celebrate the curiosity within all of your students.

8. As an extension activity, provide students the opportunity to seek answers to their questions in books and online.

Actions to Promote Curiosity in School and in Out-of-School Programs

Wonder Walk	Bring a tablet or notebook and teach children how to take notes on a walk to document wonderings and observations.
Book Club	Create a book club centered around topics that make children wonder.
Author Questions	Keep a running list of questions children would love to ask the authors of their favorite books.
Curiosity Tour	Have each child pick one question they have about the world and then go to the library together to find out answers.
Three Stories	Ask children to go around in a group and share three stories; two stories are true and one is untrue. The other children have to find out which story is untrue.
20 Questions	Play a game where one student stands in the center of a circle and picks someone to be like an animal or famous athlete. The student acts this out and the rest of the group has to figure out what or who the student is by asking yes/no questions. If the group does that before 20 questions, they win the round.

Salsa Stories

BY LULU DELACRE

Close reading is a thorough reading and rereading of text, making the process of reading visible. We demonstrate the reading process, illuminate fine writing techniques, and connect themes in support of the 7 Strengths Model.

Summary: *Salsa Stories* follows a girl named Carmen Teresa who gets a notebook for her birthday. Carmen Teresa asks her family members what she should write in her notebook. They suggest she fill it with stories from their memories of growing up. Carmen shows curiosity by listening to their stories to find out more information, and then by deciding on her own what to include in her notebook.

BEFORE READING

Discuss Curiosity:
- What do you wonder about? What big questions do you ask yourself?
- What are you curious about in your reading life before you start a new book?

Discuss the Book's Cover:
- What do you think the girl might be thinking?
- What, based on the cover, might the little girl be wondering about?

DURING READING

> "What should I write in this book?" I ask her.
> Doña Josefa's creased face lights up with her smile. "There are many things you can write," she says. "Perhaps you will want to keep a journal, like I did."

> "Or," offers Abuelita, "you could write about things that have happened to you when you were younger."
> "Yes. Or maybe, you could collect stories from our family and friends," suggests Mamá, "since everyone is here today."

Interpretation:
- Is Carmen Teresa curious? How might you know?
- What are you wondering about Carmen Teresa? What do you hope to find out about the characters?

Many years ago on a misty October afternoon in Lima, Peru, I watched Mamá bake *turrón de Doña Pepa*. Even though she made it every year before the procession for the Lord of Miracles, I had never asked her why.

"Why do you bake *turrón* in October?" I asked. "Why is this the only time they sell it all over the city?"

"*¿Por qué, por qué?*" she sighed as she sprinkled the freshly-baked nougat with tiny colorful candies. "Always asking questions, Josefa. Why? It is because this is the month of the Lord of Miracles."

Not satisfied with her answer, I continued to ask more questions. Who was Doña Pepa? And why do so many people dress in purple around this time? Finally, I wore Mamá out and she said, "I really should tell you the beautiful story that goes with the nougat. After all, you are named after its creator, Josefina Marmanillo."

Author's Craft:

- Why do you think the author included this dialogue? What does it tell us about Doña Josefa?
- Why might the author have chosen to put quotation marks around some questions but not others?

present my very own, I borrow Doña Josefa's fountain pen and open my book to the first page. Then, with great flourishes and curls, I write:

Carmen Teresa's Book of Fantastic Family Recipes

Gently, I blow on the wet ink to dry it, and I close the book. And tomorrow, I will begin collecting my recipes.

Interpretation:

- How do you think Carmen's curiosity helped her throughout the story?
- How do you think the family members felt when they saw how curious Carmen Teresa was about their stories? Why did they feel that way? What evidence in the text supports your thinking?

AFTER READING

Have you ever been curious about your family the way Carmen Teresa was about hers? What can you do to find out more about your family? How does curiosity play a role in your life? What does curiosity do to make your life more interesting?

▶ **For other favorite books on curiosity, see page 199.**

Using Technology to Promote Curiosity

- **Shadow Puppet Edu App:** Have students create a narrated slide show with questions they have about a book.

- **Family Dropbox:** Create a class or family Dropbox where students can store research projects and work on them collaboratively.

- **Voice Recorder:** Brainstorm questions you have as you read with this app.

- **Google Search:** Work with students to use online search tools to discover answers to questions. Have them refine their search queries to optimize their search results.

- **Online Resources:** Teach students how to use the online resources of public libraries and universities for their literature-related research.

What You Can Do to Promote Curiosity at Home

You have an important role in helping families encourage a healthy sense of curiosity in their children. Curiosity is really a process of inquiry, of constantly searching for answers. Families can be inspired by you to know that this requires a tremendous amount of patience and openness to the child-centered idea. A home that hopes to cultivate curiosity will need to make that space an unstructured, unrestricted time for exploration. Such a home will celebrate the journey even more than the destination.

Encourage families to follow the child's interests and curiosities and expand upon them to build a world of information around the books they read. You might have them:

- Do an Internet search about the setting of a book.
- Use a smartphone to look up unfamiliar words or phrases.
- Build background of historical events or periods mentioned in the books they read by consulting informational articles or streaming videos.
- Travel to a destination mentioned in a book or use the Internet to take a virtual tour.
- Keep a wall of wonderings.

Request that families allow time for children's uninterrupted exploration and that they encourage and celebrate a sense of wonder. Keep your homework load slim to enable families the time they need for this unstructured exploratory time, and provide families with tips about the types of tools (book bins, magazines, technology) and activities (free browsing, making collages, playing literature-based games) to make available to children to encourage this type of inquiry.

When homework is given, select assignments that promote literacy-based inquiry, such as a family research project. Encourage families to participate in meaningful discussions at home during which they encourage children to ask open-ended questions of the world and to follow up on those questions. Get families outside when possible to explore nature and to use that curiosity as a launching point for reading and writing. Create home and community scavenger hunts that connect to the books that you read. Finally, remind families that they can be role models of curious learners, lifelong explorers, and critical questioners of the world by asking open-ended questions with their children.

Curiosity lends itself to all kinds of exploration, so this is a good time to bring family "experts" to the classroom, from the mom who is a nurse practitioner to the dad who is an electrician, they can be invited in to talk about how their curiosity leads them to do well at work.

Super Reader Family Guide

Actions to Develop Your Child's Sense of Curiosity

Wonder Walk	Bring a tablet or notebook and teach your child how to take notes on wonderings and observations.
Book Basket	Create a basket of books on topics your child is wondering about.
Neighborhood Walk	Go on a walk around the neighborhood as a family and stop and jot down what you observe.
Curiosity Window	Use tape and draw a box in a window; put markers and pens and index cards near the window so your child can look out the window and take notes on what he or she sees.
Curiosity Tour	Have each family member come up with one question he or she has about the world. Then go to the library together to find out answers.
20 Questions	Ask a family member to stand in the center of a circle of people and pick someone to be, like an animal or famous athlete. Then he or she acts out the choice, while members of the group guesses what or who he or she is by asking yes and no questions. If the group members figure out what or who the family member is in 20 questions or fewer, they win the round.

Routines to Develop Your Child's Sense of Curiosity

- Keep a wonderings chart of your child's questions; go online with your child and find the answers together.

- Ask your child questions that spark meaningful conversation.

- Ignite your child's curiosity by taking him or her to a museum, park, or another place that relates to a book he or she has read.

- Have your child keep a journal of wonderings and create a story based on his or her questions.

- Encourage your child to read informational books about new or unfamiliar topics.

- Make observations about your surroundings when out and about with your child.

- On slips of paper, write down new words your child discovers and keep them in a word jar. Every now and then, take them out and discuss their meanings.

CHAPTER 5

STRENGTH 3: FRIENDSHIP

"Let there be no purpose in friendship save the deepening of the spirit."

—**KHALIL GIBRAN**

For a video snapshot of friendship in action, visit scholastic.com /superreaderresources.

Roberto and Santina are very different kinds of readers. Roberto is an English language newcomer, having recently arrived to the United States from Nepal. Reading in English feels hard for him. Santina is a fluent reader. She is from Jordan. She reads from morning until night. They are both 10 years old. Their teacher has paired them as reading partners for the week. They are studying the theme of bullying in their whole-class discussions. In their reading partnership, Roberto is reading a book called *Enemy Pie* by Derek Munson. Santina is reading R. J. Palacio's *Wonder.* These books are at very different reading levels. But Roberto and Santina can connect around the big themes of both books and back to the conversation of the whole class. At the end of the week, Roberto said to Santina, "You are a great reading friend to me." And Santina said, "I feel the same for you." Across levels, across cultures, across languages, the common themes bring them together and it is interesting to them to talk about the way the struggles of feeling ashamed or feeling lonely transcend cultures. They are united as book friends.

Maria and Iliana came from Mexico to a large elementary school in Los Angeles within a month of each other—after the school year had started. Both brought strong language skills in Spanish and had received an excellent education in their home country. Fortunately, the third-grade class they joined included 12 children who spoke Spanish and English at home, two who spoke Vietnamese, and four who spoke solely English. The majority of the children understood the benefits and beauty of being a dual language learner and knew that their home language was welcomed in the class. While listening to the teacher read aloud *In My Family: En Mi Familia* (Garza, 1996), which includes vignettes in both English and Spanish, one of the children suggested making a class book to add to the others in the library. Each child could write a vignette about their special family traditions and create a watercolor to support their writing, similar to the author's style. One student explained to Maria and Iliana, in Spanish, what the class would be creating and the joy on the girls' faces was unforgettable. Throughout the process, Maria and Iliana worked closely with their classmates to create their vignette and artwork. When it was time for each student to share their writing during Author's Chair, several chose to share in both Spanish and English. Maria and Iliana shared in Spanish and received the same applause as their peers. For the teacher, it was a profound moment when she witnessed the power of literature to bring children together and the role that reading and writing could play in developing and solidifying friendships.

Elizabeth and Gregorio are editing short films on "youth voice" that the kids have created to share with wider audiences. Over the past four weeks they have been reading literature and talking with their peers about what it means for young people to play a

powerful and positive role in social change. Although they are very young, Elizabeth already has the reputation of being a great filmmaker. "Lizzy," "Lizzy," you can hear throughout the room as other kids want Lizzy's advice on their final editorial decisions. The films are due to be shown THE NEXT DAY! Gregorio doesn't call out to Lizzy. Instead he looks at the iMovie clips on his laptop with his head in his hands. He is at the breaking point and there is no doubt he is considering an early retirement from the filmmaking profession. But Lizzy sees him and walks across the room and begins to speak to him in reassuring whispers. The expression on Gregorio's face changes as Lizzy reassures him that his film will be fine (which it is!). As she returns to her seat and puts her headphones back on to edit her own film, Lizzy is beaming. Her teacher gives her the subtle thumbs-up and she nods like "I know. I'm the champ." That next day all of the kids' short films are shown to great acclaim, including Gregorio's. Lizzy's film becomes a brief Internet sensation receiving thousands of views on Facebook and YouTube.

Why Friendship Matters

Educational psychologist Robert Selman has devoted much of his career to understanding friendship and its importance to children's social and emotional health and well-being. Selman's Five Stages of Friendship Development are described in his 2007 book, *The Promotion of Social Awareness: Powerful Lessons From the Partnership Between Developmental Theory and Classroom Practice*. Selman believes that the essence of friendship development is perspective taking, or the ability of young people to take into consideration other people's points of view. Over time, as children learn to see those points of view and integrate them with their own, they are better able to manage relationships in their lives. In order to promote a vibrant community of learners, of super readers, in the classroom, in the home, or in the world, children need to learn the skill of perspective taking and they need to be given plenty of opportunities in class and at home to practice that skill.

What You Can Do to Promote Friendship in School and in Out-of-School Programs

Use literature to recognize the power, work, and complexities of friendship.

The power and magnificence of friendship courses its way through the greatest literature of our times, both classic and contemporary. Across cultures, languages, customs, and traditions, friendship's lasting value to society is clear. What we have not always recognized in the classroom, however, is how powerful it can be to academic development.

A first grader who reads *Mr. Putter and Tabby* learns about the gentle, life-affirming purpose of friendship. A third grader who reads *The Stories Julian Tells* and discusses the tender and evocative moments of connection. The fifth grader who reads *The Lightning Thief* for book club is excited to find that friendship can be complex and adventurous. The middle schooler can disappear into the Hunger Games series, finding that boys and girls can have friendships that may be more layered than they could have imagined.

Books such as those are guides, explorations, and exhilarations, helping children to navigate the most important connections of humanity. It is also interesting to study cultural similarities and differences about friendship, in spite of poverty, deep challenges, and separations. Your library collection should promote discussions, values, and inquiry related to friendship. Study good friendships in books as well as bumpy ones, for the bumpy ones can teach children how to be better friends and how to navigate hard parts with mutual respect and positive feelings. Have changing baskets that the children label based on books they are reading independently that bring texture to the study of friendship, such as:

- friendships that last a long time
- friendships that face trouble
- friendships that are complicated
- friendships that are comforting/inspiring
- friendship role models/heroes

Work collaboratively to grow ideas.

People rely on one another to overcome obstacles and challenges, and friendship is so much a part of that. When Pam's father was sick in the hospital, she received a text from her friend Elizabeth: "I've come to the hospital. I know it's late, so I am going to be here in my car outside waiting, in case you should need me." In our classrooms, when children are working through big ideas, the hard work of reading, or seeking to write something, we must seize opportunities to celebrate, affirm, and cultivate collaboration that comes from trusting friendships.

Compare the friendships in stories you read to the work of the classroom. Use the friendship role models you find in texts to inform your teaching of classroom values. "We saw how Anne and Diana stood up for each other in *Anne of Green Gables*. We saw how Frog and Toad are steady friends to each other, rain or shine. How can we do the same while supporting our friends as they work through hard problems or difficult moments as readers or writers?" Here are some practical ways to form partnerships among super readers in the classroom:

- Show children how to be careful listeners and supporters of each other's work by providing concrete language: "I admire the way you worked through the hard part of that story." "I liked the idea you had about that problem."

- Create weekly partnerships that are formed based on things other than reading levels, perhaps similar questions the children have about what they are reading, or similar interests in genre or writing type, or around passion for certain topics.

- Set up "Friendship Quests" where you encourage children to pair up with a "new" friend in the class, someone they do not know as well, and have them do a fun problem together, write a story together, or listen online to a story and record each other in a mini-interview talking about the book.

- In shared online documents and blogs, have students coauthor responses to texts and ideas they've been building. There are children who will prefer to nurture friendships in writing or by exchanging snippets of audio or video. In the "old" days, these children would have been considered shy and they perhaps had fewer friends. But today, those same children have the chance to have active, "talkative" lives of learning and collaboration with the support of online technologies.

Build a powerful community through friendship.

We can cultivate friendships through active forms of literacy such as singing, reciting poetry, engaging in group projects, participating in collective writing projects, journaling to one another, having e-pals, and celebrating/respecting other opinions about texts. Reader and writer's theater, bringing to life picture books, chapter books, poetry, and even informational texts can bring out children's inner lives, stories, and strengths, lifting academics up off the page and into the spirit of community. Illuminate the fact that you will celebrate a child who reaches out to another child for friendship. Admire the super reader who initiates:

- A Friendship Lunch—bringing a lunch for a friend and a book to share.
- A book exchange at holiday time.
- A special section of the classroom library called "Recommended by a Friend."
- Friend Chats About Books, which can happen any time of day, from recess to the minutes after children arrive at school. Keep cards or sticky notes handy, or if you are doing this online, a special place for recording what the chat was about.

Friendship Chain

By analyzing their own experiences with friendly relationships and those of characters in books, you can encourage super readers' to reflect on the importance of friendship to their community.

Directions

1. **Introduce the lesson by saying:**

   The good relationships we have with others often have some characteristics in common. There are things that good friends do to make others feel positive and like they belong. Today we are going to create Friendship Chains. These chains will help us to identify the positive things we can do to be good friends and will help us recognize the people who are and have been amazing friends to us!

2. **Cut pieces of construction paper into long strips. Give each student a handful. Explain to students they will write an action of a good friend on one side of a paper strip—for example: "Friends stand up for you." On the other side, have them write the name of a real person or a fictional character they know who has carried out that action. You can say:**

   Let's take a few minutes to brainstorm some of the things good friends do. For example, friends stand up for you, friends cheer you up when you're feeling down (you may want to write these examples on the board for students to see). On each of your strips, you're going to write down one of these actions. On the back of the strip, you can write down the names of people or characters you have observed who have acted in this way! For example, you could write, "Friends help each other be brave." On the back, you could write, "In Charlotte's Web, Charlotte helped Wilbur be brave."

3. Encourage students to write as many strips as they can. If they think of many people who have completed the same action, they may write them all on separate strips of paper. Encourage them to be specific in the actions they identify.

4. Once students have created their strips, ask them to staple them into links to create a chain that can be displayed somewhere prominently.

5. Have students share some of the actions they wrote down and discuss some of the most common ones. Connect these actions to students' interactions within their reading community. Ask them, "How can acting this way help us make our reading community stronger?"

Actions to Promote Friendship in School and in Out-of-School Programs

Friendship Collage	Have students create a collage celebrating powerful elements of friendship with different kinds of images (a lion photo for example to demonstrate fierce loyalty, etc.).
Friendship Memory Book	Invite students to create a friendship book where they collect their favorite memories of their friends during the school year.
Friendship Bill of Rights	Invite students to draft a list of 10 qualities they strive to have as a good friend.
Bookmark Buddies	Ask students to create their own bookmarks by drawing an image of a book character they believe would be a good friend in real life. Encourage them to use the bookmarks and take the characters on their upcoming journeys through new books.
Friendship Circle	At the end of the day (or when your schedule allows), have everyone sit in a circle and share one way the person seated beside them has been a good friend.

CLOSE READING LESSON

Those Shoes

BY MARIBETH BOELTS
ILLUSTRATED BY NOAH Z. JONES

Close reading is a thorough reading and rereading of text, making the process of reading visible. We demonstrate the reading process, illuminate fine writing techniques, and connect themes in support of the 7 Strengths Model.

Summary: *Those Shoes* follows two boys, Anthony and Jeremy, who both want a pair of shoes that everyone at school has. Anthony and Jeremy both learn what it means to be a good friend when Jeremy gets the coveted shoes.

BEFORE READING	**Discuss Friendship:**

BEFORE READING

Discuss Friendship:
- What feels important to you about friendship?
- What are one or two of the most important things a friend does to support you?

Discuss the Book's Cover:
- What do you notice about the illustration?
- What themes might be in this book based on the cover?
- What does the cover tell you about the relationships between characters?

DURING READING

Interpretation:
- What kind of friend might Antonio be and how do you know that?
- Why do you think Antonio is the only one who doesn't laugh?

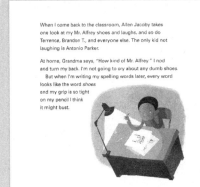

Author's Craft:

What does this illustration inspire in you about friendship?

Before I can change my mind, the shoes are in my coat. Snow is beginning to fall as I run across the street to Antonio's apartment. I put the shoes in front of his door, push the doorbell—and run.

AFTER READING

Which characters in the story showed friendship? How did they show friendship? How did some characters not show friendship? Why do you think the author included those characters?

What did you find out about Jeremy's character? What is the author's message about friendship?

How could you be a good friend? In what ways is friendship important in your life?

▶ For other favorite books on friendship, see page 200.

Using Technology to Promote Friendship

- **Email:** Help students craft messages to friends and family members about their favorite books.

- **Google Hangout:** Let children connect with friends and family members to share what they are reading. Encourage a child to develop a digital-pal relationship with a family member who lives far away to talk about the books that they like.

- **Goodreads:** Join and find like-minded friends who love similar types of texts.

- **Digital Pals:** Arrange for students to be digital pals with a classroom in a different community or country. Use face-to-face communication tools like FaceTime, Google Hangout, or Skype to facilitate conversations.

What You Can Do to Promote Friendship at Home

The type of work you do in promoting relationship building and budding friendships at school can be done by families at home, too. The home and the community are ideal places to teach children the value and work of friendship and to begin to connect friendship to becoming super readers.

Encourage families to choose books to read with their children that highlight friendship. Stress the importance of talking productively with their children about what it means to be a good friend. You can help families model friendship by sharing sentence starters with them about the characteristics of good friendship like empathy, concern, being a good listener, or showing support. Provide questions such as the following:

- When have you felt like a good friend?

- When has being a friend felt hard?

- What are the qualities of good friends?

Families can also form family or neighborhood book or storytelling clubs that encourage friendships around reading and sharing great books. With technologies like Google Hangout, Skype, WhatsApp, and FaceTime, kids and families can create virtual book chats with distant relatives and friends in other parts of the world. This takes some planning, so consider giving families specific instructions or assignments that will encourage those activities.

Super Reader Family Guide

Actions to Develop Your Child's Sense of Friendship

Friendship Collage
Create a collage where you identify with your child admirable traits in his or her family members and friends.

Friendship Memory Book
Invite your child to create a friendship book where he or she collects favorite memories with family members and friends.

Family and Friends Dinner
Organize a dinner where each family member invites a friend.

Friendship Chain
Cut pieces of paper into strips. On each strip, have a family member write down a way he or she is a good friend, and a way others are good friends to him or her. Link the strips by taping or stapling the ends together to make a Friendship Chain.

Friendship Circle
At the end of the day (or as schedules allow), have family members and friends sit in a circle and share one way the person seated beside them has been a good friend.

Routines to Develop Your Child's Sense of Friendship

- Read books around the theme of friendship with your child.

- Model reading behaviors for book clubs or with book buddies.

- Ask your child to share his or her favorite books.

CHAPTER 6

STRENGTH 4: KINDNESS

"We carry with us, as human beings, not just the capacity to be kind, but the very choice of kindness."

—R. J. PALACIO, from *Wonder*

Like clockwork, at 10:30 each day, Matthew would open the door to the third-grade classroom, look around, and cautiously step inside. He towered over most of the children, at least by a foot, and was painfully shy and quiet.

 For a video snapshot of kindness in action, visit scholastic.com /superreaderresources.

Initially, he was embarrassed to come to the class as a fourth grader, but his special education teacher and the third-grade teacher thought he would thrive in a class doing math at his level with a hands-on, project-based learning approach. And like clockwork, the teacher would smile and the room would erupt with enthusiastic phrases including "Hi, Matthew!" "Here's a seat!" and "Come sit with us today!" The daily ritual took about 30 seconds from the time he stepped into the room until he found a seat. However, the overwhelming impact of so many positive words and genuine kindness could not be measured. Did Matthew grow as a mathematician that year? By leaps and bounds. Was his academic growth connected to how he was treated? Most likely. He knew he was welcomed, he knew we cared about him, and small words and acts of kindness blossomed into friendships at recess and in the classroom.

Marisol, age 10, wrote in her notebook that because of her time in foster care she had never had a birthday party. She wrote about what she'd wish for at a party if she had one— a big beautiful white cream cake with pink frosting, a music playlist with all her favorite mariachi songs, and yellow and orange and pink balloons. She read this story aloud to her class and soon after, members of the class approached us. "We'd like to make Marisol the birthday party she never had," they told us. And so, they and their families took action. They decorated the room with yellow and orange and pink balloons. They made a cake, white cream of course, with pink frosting. They created a playlist with all her favorite songs. Marisol and her friends danced and sang. The act of kindness shown by her classmates drew from her own story and from the kind of environment that valued the telling and sharing of personal stories. Kindness is an act of social justice. Children can learn in everyday ways how personal stories can fuel the power of kindness and how kindness can change the world. Marisol was

touched by the kindness of her friends but also her friends were touched by Marisol's story. And Marisol got to tell a new story after that day, a story emblematic of the 7 Strengths classroom, where reading one's own stories and writing down one's own life makes a difference.

Why Kindness Matters

Children enter the educational system with a wealth of experiences. And while we wish it were otherwise, many students have not had the benefits of an intellectually nurturing environment. The major inhibitors of learning—stress, abuse, trauma—can be all too present in a child's early years. Research out of Harvard University's Center on the Developing Child shows that though a child's temperament and early experiences may affect his or her learning initially, the cumulative impact of positive experiences make it easier for him or her to achieve positive outcomes (National Scientific Council on the Developing Child, 2015). Programs that incorporate meaningful connections between staff and students, as well between student and student, contribute significantly to this development of resilience.

Nel Noddings observes in her book *Happiness and Education* that children and adults alike learn best when they are happy, while sustained stress can physically alter the neural connections of the brain. Creating a positive learning environment for children can combat traumatic or detrimental experiences such as child abuse, poverty, malnourishment, or family and community violence that may hinder their learning. "Brain research reveals superior learning takes place when classroom experiences are relevant to students' lives, interests, and experiences."

Cultivating supportive relationships within the classroom is the first step to fostering super readers who will impact the world beyond it. One key ingredient to creating these types of spaces is kindness. When adults and peers model and encourage kindness, children come to appreciate how it feels to be treated with kindness and the joy that comes from extending kindness to others (2003).

What You Can Do to Promote Kindness in School and in Out-of-School Programs

Value tenderness.

There are many ways a reading community can value tenderness. First, be sure there are examples of tenderness in the texts you are reading—in picture books, chapter books, informational texts, and poems. In the picture book *Stevie* by John Steptoe, two characters find ways to express kindness for each other, even though one at first feels supplanted by the other. In the chapter book *Wonder*, a boy with a facial disfigurement connects with others. Through informational texts, children can learn about kindness. In *Koko's Kitten*, for example, the author shares a special bond between a large gorilla and a kitten. In *14 Cows for America*, Carmen Agra Deedy shows the breathtaking way a small African village makes an enormous impact with a very special gift following the events of September 11th.

Studying point of view in literature can have a far-reaching influence on a child's ability to respect perspectives that may be different from his or her own. When we give children opportunities, through literature to witness the other side of a story or the internal struggle of a beloved character, we arm them with knowledge about the complexities of our social world. The more children experience a love of character, the more they develop the muscle to love one another—and become super readers.

In the classroom, value tenderness by showing you care about it. Create a Kindness Box to which children can add a note whenever they spot an act of kindness. Throw a celebration when the box is full. Have a Kindness Hero of the Week; celebrate characters in books who demonstrate kindness. In *Leadership: The Power of Emotional Intelligence*, Daniel Goleman stresses the importance of having leaders who can demonstrate cognitive and emotional empathy. He explains: "Because you understand other perspectives, you can put things in ways colleagues comprehend. And you welcome their questions, just to be sure. Cognitive empathy, along with reading another person's feelings accurately, makes for effective communication." In other words, kindness and tenderness are not "soft skills." They are crucial to creating future leaders, as well as super readers.

Make time for affirmation.

Recognize acts of kindness. Make role models of students who exhibit empathy regularly. Be aware, though, often those students are the ones who are not noticed—they are the ones who let everyone else "go first," give things away, don't compete with others, and are not the first to raise their hands. It often takes an astute teacher to notice and value empathy. Make public compliments that affirm those children:

- Thank you, John, for making it possible for Sarah to speak first.
- I want to appreciate Gabriella and Jeremy for demonstrating strong and caring partnership skills today.
- I saw that the box of paper clips fell to the ground and Emily and Hakim took the lead in cleaning it up and I want to compliment them on that.

Explore the role of kindness as an interpersonal asset.

One child reading to another child is in its own way a powerful act of kindness. Organize cross-grade-level partner read alouds for World Read Aloud Day, which happens in midwinter every year. Reach across cultural divides by sharing read alouds with partner schools through videoconference calls or Internet chats.

Partnerships like those are beautiful ways to help children practice kindness; it is how they become strong partners, how they learn to be supportive and kind speakers and listeners who pause intentionally and value the small moves people make when they are affirming one another. Praise is so easy to offer and often so easily overlooked. Help children by setting the stage for a life of kindness.

Offer language that super readers can use with one another, such as:

- What I think you are saying is…

- I really admire the hard work you did today as a reader.

- I enjoyed working with you today.

- I'd like to help you…

- How can I be of support?

When we are kind, we take people seriously, no matter their age. We need to teach children the skill of active speaking and listening and help them build definitions of what a culture of kindness means to them.

Role Models of Kindness

By guiding super readers to celebrate kindness in people and characters they admire, you can encourage them to reflect on the importance of this strength to members of a reading community.

Directions

1. **Introduce the lesson by saying:**

Today we are going to create Role Models of Kindness. We will start by thinking about people whose kindness was important to their success. When we think about role models, sometimes it's easy to focus on accomplishments and forget about the qualities that made them possible. One quality that many of our role models have is kindness, and that's a big reason we look up to them!

2. **Ask the students to think about some of the figures they look up to. You can say:**

For a few minutes, let's all think about people we look up to. This can be a real person, someone from history, or it can be a character in a book. Just make sure you choose someone whose kindness played a big role in his or her life and success.

3. **Offer some examples to help clarify this for students. You can say:**

Let's talk about some examples of people who exemplify kindness: Malala Yousafzai is a Kindness Role Model. She is a Pakistani girl who stood up for the right of all girls to get an education. Even after the Taliban attacked her, she continued to stand up for what she believed in. Malala demonstrates kindness and compassion every day as she champions girls around the world. Hermione Granger from the Harry Potter series is a Kindness Role Model. Throughout the books, Hermione is a smart and brave character. However, she is also very kind to the people around her, and supportive of Harry and Ron no matter what adventures or challenges come their way.

4. **After discussing these examples, give the students time to think of their own Kindness Role Models, and write about why kindness was important to their success.**

   - Tell them they don't need to write a lot, just two or three sentences.
   - Halfway through the allotted time, explain that students may use the figures you suggested if they have trouble thinking of their own. If they do so, ask them to try to think about other ways those figures are kind.

5. Once each student has chosen a figure and written a little bit about him or her, distribute unlined sheets of paper. Invite students to draw the people they chose, and to include what they wrote about them as well. You can say:

Now we will create posters to celebrate our Kindness Role Models. On your sheet of paper, you will each draw a picture of the person you chose, and the explanation you wrote down. You can make your poster look however you want. You can draw a big picture with a caption, or have big text and a small image to go with it. The designing and decorating is up to you. Just remember to include your Kindness Role Model's name!

6. Be sure to leave a few minutes for sharing student work and discussing the activity, and praise everyone for creating their posters and sharing their ideas. Guiding questions might include:

   - Did you learn about any new kindness role models today? What is one that impressed you and why?

   - Why might kindness be necessary as we read and learn together? Name specific situations where kindness would be important.

   - When does kindness break down in school or clubs? Why?

   - How can we help each other remember to be kind?

7. As an extension activity, have students write down one way they can bring what they learned from the Kindness Role Model lesson that they can bring into the reading community. Post their writing in the classroom.

8. As a homework extension activity, encourage families to research the child's Kindness Role Model together. Ask adults and children at home to share who their Kindness Role Models are.

Actions to Promote Kindness in School and in Out-of-School Programs

Kindness Webs	Create webs based on the books you read. Have students give each character his or her own circle, and then draw lines to connect the characters who have been kind to each other. Students can write a description of each kind act along the lines.
Kindness in Action	Create a running list of kindness actions you see others doing, from the children to the adults in the school, that you can add to continually, and emulate where possible.
Kindness Hall of Fame	Look for examples of kindness in books read together and post them on a Kindness Hall of Fame.
Messages of Kindness	Invite everyone to write kind, anonymous messages to students in the class that you distribute.

Freak the Mighty

BY RODMAN PHILBRICK

Close reading is a thorough reading and rereading of text, making the process of reading visible. We demonstrate the reading process, illuminate fine writing techniques, and connect themes in support of the 7 Strengths Model.

Summary: *Freak the Mighty* tells the story of Max, a kind boy with a learning disability, and Kevin, a physically disadvantaged genius. Both characters are faced with unique challenges, but they team up to become best friends. The book follows their many adventures and hardships in New Hampshire.

BEFORE READING	**Discuss Kindness:** • Why is it important to be kind to strangers as well as to friends? **Discuss the Book's Cover:** • What do you notice about the two characters? • What do the colors and mood of the cover indicate to you about possible themes in the book?
DURING READING	**Interpretation:** • Put yourself in Freak's place. What is going through your mind?

> because he can't see. There are so many people crowded around, all he can see are feet and knees, and people are lifting their little kids up to see the fireworks explode like hot pink flowers in the sky, and so I just sort of reach down without thinking and pick up Freak and set him on my shoulders.

Author's Craft:

- What lines do you like? What does the author do with punctuation and word choice to help reveal the character?

> "Maybe we should reconsider this particular quest," Freak says. He's up there on my shoulders and he's getting fidgety, squirming around.
>
> But we're already outside the apartment door, and I go, "Maybe she really needs that ID card," so it's my fault what happens next.

Interpretation:

- What did you learn about Freak from his dictionary?
- Do you think Max and Freak are kind to each other? Why or why not?

Freak seems like he's just as excited as me, even though he already knows what he put inside. "Take off all the paper first," he says. "There's a special way to open it."

Real careful, I peel off all the paper, and the thing is, it's not a pyramid-shaped box he bought somewhere, he *made* it. You can see where he cut out the pieces of cardboard and taped them all together, and written on the sides of the pyramid are these little signs and arrows.

"Follow the arrows," he says.

The arrows point all over the place and I have to keep turning the pyramid around, until finally I get to this sign that says:

PRESS HERE AND BE AMAZED

"Go on," Freak says. "It's not an explosive device, silly — it won't blow up in your face."

I press the spot on the pyramid and all of a sudden, all four sides fold down at the same time and I'm looking inside the pyramid and, just like Freak promised, I'm amazed.

"The young man is a genius," Grim is saying. "And I don't use that word lightly."

Grim is right about that, because Freak has the whole thing rigged with these elastic bands and paper clips, which is what made the sides unfold all at the same time, and inside is this little platform and on the platform is a book. Not a normal book, like you buy in the store, but a book he made himself, you can tell that right away. It looks so special, I'm afraid to pick it up or I might ruin it.

"What I did was take all my favorite words," Freak says, "and put them in alphabetical order."

"Like a dictionary?"

"Exactly," Freak says, "but different, because this is *my* dictionary. Go on and look inside."

AFTER READING

- How does Max and Freak's friendship help them throughout the book?
- How have you shown kindness? How did it help the other person?
- What might the author's message be in relation to kindness? What might we take away as an action step?

▶ For other favorite books on kindness, see page 200.

What You Can Do to Promote Kindness at Home

You can help your families use reading, writing, and discussion to think about and plan ways they can use kindness to affect the world around them.

Encourage families to provide opportunities for children to see themselves demonstrating kindness in the home, in the community, and in the larger world. An older sibling can become a reading buddy with a younger brother or sister. Children may use FaceTime to become reading buddies with a distant aunt, uncle, or grandparent. Perhaps families can volunteer to do community service together such as reading to sight-impaired residents of a nursing home, writing letters to soldiers, or tutoring at the library.

Suggest that families host kindness conversations. Families can talk with children about social problems that they see in their community and in the larger society, and they can discuss as a family what they might do to help solve those problems. Remind families to listen to their children in these conversations and to honor the opinions and perspectives they bring to the discussions.

Encourage families to find innovative ways to measure and reward acts of kindness in the home and in the community. Families can model kindness in everyday social interactions, and they can help children understand that kindness is more than being nice, it is also a genuine concern for others and a way of using reading, writing, listening, and speaking to improve the world in some way. Some of the best examples of kindness are those closest to home. Suggest to families that when a child kisses a baby sibling goodnight or helps his or her grandmother to bring the food to the table, these are kindness moments. You might even consider sending home kindness star stickers for families to use when they "catch" a child in an act of quiet kindness.

Super Reader Family Guide

Actions to Develop Your Child's Sense of Kindness

Kindness Webs	Create webs based on the books you read. Give each character his or her own circle, and then draw lines to connect the characters who have been kind to each other. Write a description of each kind act along the lines.
Kindness in Action	Create a running list of kindness actions that you and your child can add to continually, and take action on one each week.
Kindness Hall of Fame	Look for examples of kindness in books you and your child read together and post them on a Kindness Hall of Fame.
Messages of Kindness	Invite family members to write kind, anonymous messages to each other.
I Am Kind	Have everyone choose one small way to demonstrate kindness to the rest of the family and commit to doing it!

Routines to Develop Your Child's Sense of Kindness

- Borrow books from friends, family, or the local library. Demonstrate the proper care of others' property.

- Let your child know when someone showed you kindness, and how it made you feel.

- Help your child keep track of acts of kindness he or she receives.

- Encourage your child to do an act of kindness each day, and then post a "kindness star" on the refrigerator with the child's good deed written on it.

- Talk about digital citizenship. What does it feel like when someone is being kind to you online? When have you expressed kindness online?

- Find out if your local library offers programs that teach reading skills. If it does, volunteer as a family.

- Encourage your child to practice good listening and speaking skills when sharing books and toys with others.

- Develop a philanthropy project with your child inspired by a character in a book.

- Have your child start a blog showing ways to be kind and promoting acts of kindness.

CHAPTER 7

STRENGTH 5: CONFIDENCE

"I am not afraid of storms, for I am learning how to sail my ship."
—**LOUISA MAY ALCOTT, from** *Little Women*

When Tripp was about three and a half years old, he was sitting on his bed with his mom and she said to him, "Read to me!" He looked up from one of his favorite books, *Dragons Love Tacos*, laughed, and said, "I don't know how to read! Read to me!" At the tender age of three, he already understood what it meant to decode the words on the page, to use his voice to represent various characters and moods, and draw meaning from the illustrations. However, he also understood that he did not yet know how to attach the right sounds to the letters to read the exact words on the page. For a three-year-old, we may be surprised at his understanding of reading and appreciate his continued confidence in his development as a reader.

In a fourth-grade classroom in San Francisco, filled with desks for 32 children, bookshelves, computers, a pet hamster named Percy, book boxes, file cabinets, and a slew of art materials, the teacher is wondering where to move that one boy who continues to talk and disrupt his classmates. She knows he is having difficulty reading the textbooks, which have jumped in complexity and vocabulary, with fewer illustrations and photos to provide support. There are only so many ways to configure 32 desks in a space reasonably large enough for 25. As soon as it's independent work time, the talking and distracting behavior starts. She moved him by Percy but he continued to talk to Percy and disrupted the rest of the students. He is a sweet child, rather shy, and she knows teachers are not supposed to have favorites, but he is one of hers. She finally decides to sit him by her desk, but he is frustrated and angry and

> For a video snapshot of confidence in action, visit scholastic.com /superreaderresources.

refuses to move. Before she can ask him one more time to move, he yells, "I CAN'T READ!" The room is silenced. This is not news to his teacher or peers.

The three-year-old and the fourth grader are aware of themselves as readers. They understand reading's ability to open or limit access to information or enjoyment depending on the ability of the reader. The three-year-old is amused at being directed to read because he is not being judged on his ability to read. The fourth grader, who has been in school for four full years and two months, is acutely aware of himself as a reader. By the end of the school year, the fourth grader was reading and writing nearly at grade level, thanks to intense after-school tutoring with his teacher. Both boys have the ability to learn and thrive and become successful readers. The three-year-old is confident in his ability to grow but for a fourth grader, after years of watching peers develop as readers and move so far ahead of him, it is reasonable to see why he has lost confidence. Confidence leads to risk taking, which leads to growth. How can we ensure that children grow in their confidence as they continue to grow in their competence? We nurture both.

Why Confidence Matters

Often schools perceive unmotivated readers as kids who do not value reading when the real problem is that the students lack confidence in themselves as readers. When students' confidence as readers increases so does their motivation and, ultimately, their reading achievement. Recent studies by Gallup (2014) and the ACT (2014) reveal that students' educational aspirations are universally high regardless of income or background. Students want to succeed and they generally know that becoming an accomplished reader—a super reader— is important to their futures. Social psychologists who study motivation tell us that what often separates motivated readers from unmotivated ones is that the latter group lacks the confidence, or the expectation of success in the reading enterprise (Eccles & Wigfield, 2002).

In *When Kids Can't Read: What Teachers Can Do*, Kylene Beers (2003) describes three types of confidences that successful readers need. 1) *Cognitive Confidence:* They need to comprehend the text, they need to monitor their understanding, and they need to read with fluency. 2) *Social and Emotional Confidence:* They need to be willing and active participants in a community of learners, they must read for enjoyment and information, and they must have a positive attitude toward reading. 3) *Stamina and Enjoyment:* They need the stamina and confidence to continue reading difficult texts and they need the confidence that they can successfully navigate books that are of interest to them. When teachers and families are able to improve these confidences, they are also able to increase students' reading achievement and, perhaps more importantly, they help to develop students' identities as capable and engaged readers.

What You Can Do to Promote Confidence in School and in Out-of-School Programs

Tap the power of literature to help children find their confidence.

Literature inspires confidence by showing children how they can move from not thinking they can do something to knowing they can do it, that the impossible can be possible. Sometimes it seems that every book ever written is in some way about this idea, that literature is helping us travel those sometimes lonely journeys of our minds, where we are asking: "Can I make it through?" And a character, or a real-life hero, answers to us: "Yes! You can."

Here are some ways particular kinds of text help build confidence in super readers:

- Books about ordinary characters getting through tough spots, and those daily challenges of childhood, sometimes funny ones and sometimes very serious ones. Books like the Edward books by Rosemary Wells to *A Chair for My Mother* by Vera B. Williams to *The One in the Middle Is the Green Kangaroo* by Judy Blume show children mastering confidence in a variety of ways.

- Stories about real-life heroes in which their childhoods are explored and we understand that they were not born confident. They had to make their way in sometimes challenging places to achieve their sense of self. These books include

I Am Malala by Malala Yousafzai and Christina Lamb and *Mountains Beyond Mountains* (adapted for young people) by Tracy Kidder and Michael French.

- Fantasy stories and/or comics in which characters triumph over seemingly insurmountable odds through a nurturing of their own confidence—books like *The Hunger Games* by Suzanne Collins or *Song of the Lioness* by Tamora Pierce.

- Informational articles that help children see moments of confidence including interviews with athletes, conversations with scientists pursuing an idea, and sharings of writers talking about how they have to work their way through insecurity and their lack of confidence. Recently, the writer Ta-Nehesi Coates said in an interview in *The Atlantic:* "When I was done with that book, it was clear to me it was not something I could have done before. Breakthroughs come from putting…pressure on yourself and hoping you will grow some new muscles. It's not mystical….it is repeated practice over and over and you become something you had no idea you could really be.

Focus on the role of speaking and listening in a super reader's life.

Confidence is a lot about having your own voice in response to things and trusting in that voice. Children are practicing this from the start. Let us create classrooms where children have a great deal of opportunity to voice alternative viewpoints, to engage in genuine debates, to add new ideas to a conversation in an atmosphere of enjoyment and comfort. Confidence grows through active speaking and also active listening, the capacity to hear another's point of view and not be intimidated by it. Students can learn from leadership techniques to boost their own confidence, studying great leaders' speeches and interviews on YouTube and analyzing where the speaker/leader showed confidence and what strategies led him or her there.

So, too, the super reader is unafraid to ask an open-ended question herself. The best questions often do not have one answer but lead the conversation in interesting directions Conversations about texts are a great way to practice confidence building, hearing one's own voice, and putting ideas into the world. You can model sentence starters that encourage all classmates to recognize their own confidence and to bolster it in others:

- I want to hear more of what you are thinking.

- Can we add onto your big idea?

- I like what you are saying about this text. Can you say more?

- I would like to respectfully challenge your idea with my own, and then let me hear more from you.

Recognize the power of collaboration in building confidence.

A community supports trying and recognizes the fact that sometimes failing builds a child's confidence. Partners and small groups make it possible for shy children to express their views. The use of Turn and Talk and Stop and Jot can also be extremely helpful in getting those quiet voices going. (See Chapter 12 for more information on those techniques.) And really valuing listening as an art form also contributes to a quiet child's confidence. Sometimes the most talented leaders are the best listeners. Schools don't always value that skill, although it is highly regarded by all the state standards. Listening to the read aloud or listening to one another should be prized and affirmed. When we use statements like these, we send a message that we value children who are creating successful structures with their active listening stance:

- I love the way you leaned in during that Turn and Talk.

- You really noted the writer's craft in the read aloud because you were deeply listening.

- You were a great partner today because you made it possible for your partner to go deep in her thinking.

In this era, performance-based work is valued and provides an opportunity to build readers' confidence. Giving children a chance to design and build something that may take many attempts to get right builds their confidence. The "failures" are natural and normal and will require new research, note-taking, and conversations each time in order to improve the work. In our test-driven society, we sometimes act like there is only one answer and it has to come "on demand." A super reader quickly finds that most learning happens in a collaborative way. Think of our young people finding their first apartments after college, and the roommates putting together their furniture—do it yourself! It is daunting and frustrating, but also confidence building: "We can do it!" The classroom can and should be more like that, as children read manuals, read directions, put on plays, write shows, and build projects.

CONFIDENCE FOCUS LESSON

Your Own Superheroes

By having super readers create their own superheroes, you can encourage them to develop the confidence they need to be independent thinkers and express their ideas boldly.

Directions

1. Introduce the lesson by leading a conversation with your students about confidence. Ask students what confidence means to them. Feel free to use LitWorld's definition to inform your discussion: *Thinking independently and expressing ideas with assurance.*

2. Explain to students that they will now create superhero versions of themselves. You can say:

    Thank you all for sharing your thoughts on confidence. I loved hearing your ideas! Now, I want you to keep that conversation in mind for our next activity: we're all going to create superhero versions of ourselves! I think all of you are superheroes. You are all powerful in your own way, and you should have the confidence to show it when we read and learn together.

3. Tell students they will answer four questions about themselves as superheroes before creating their final Superhero Profiles. Read the questions aloud, and also be sure to write them somewhere in the room where students can read them. You can say:

    First, let's all quietly imagine superheroes in our heads. (Give them 30 seconds to use their imaginations.) *Now, picture yourself as a superhero! I know that might feel hard, so I'm going to give you four questions to think about:*

    - What does your superhero-self look like?
    - What are your superpowers?
    - Who is your sidekick or the person who helps you fight your battles?
    - What injustice do you fight? What problems do you solve?

Clarify each question by discussing them in-depth and providing an example for each. You can say:

For the first question, think about yourself as a superhero. Include your costume and something that represents you as a superhero. You should show off your superpowers, or the reasons you are confident. I'm drawing myself with big ears because I'm a great listener. My hero has hearts all over the costume because I am super-kind.

For the second question, it's okay to include fantasy superpowers like "flying" or "invisibility," but also be sure to include some superpowers that help you as a learner and reading community member, for example, "I can travel through time, but one of my learning superpowers is being great at remembering facts and details."

For the third question, think about your sidekick. How do you two work together? How do they support you? My sidekick is my little brother. He has big muscles because he is strong and protective. He always has my back.

For the last question, focus on real injustices and problems that might occur in learning communities like ours.

4. Once students have had time to answer these questions, help them create their Superhero Profiles. Each student should divide a sheet of paper into four sections, then draw and write in them based on his or her responses to the four questions. As you explain the activity, walk them through an example you have prepared in advance. You can say:

Thank you everyone for doing some great brainstorming for your superheroes. Now we're ready for the next step! I'm going to give each of you a sheet of paper that you can divide into four sections for the four questions.

You can now draw and write in each section to show your Superhero selves! The top left square is for question one, the top right square is for question two, the bottom left square is for question three, and the bottom right square is for question four.

Now, everyone can start drawing and creating their Superhero Profiles. I can't wait to see them all!

5. Once the Superhero Profiles are completed, invite students to share them. Depending on time and other constraints, you can have students share with the class, in small groups, or in pairs.

6. After students have had the chance to share, lead a discussion about the activity. Some guiding questions include:

   - How did it feel to create a superhero version of yourself?
   - Did anything surprise you about your Superhero Profile?

- How did you decide on your superpowers?
- Did you learn something about another student from his or her Superhero Profile?
- How can you bring your confident Superhero Profile to life in our reading community?

7. Be sure to thank students for a wonderful job on their Superhero Profiles, and for a great discussion! Tell them that they are all truly superheroes for being brave and sharing about themselves.

8. As a homework extension activity, ask students to interview family members and have them talk about people who are "superheroes" to them.

Actions to Promote Confidence in School and in Out-of-School Programs

I'm Proud of Me	Have students write down three reasons why they are proud of themselves.
Power Booster	Have the students write down how they will boost their confidence when they feel nervous or insecure. They do not have to share their Power Boosters, but they should use them in the future!
Constant Confidence	Build confidence as readers and speakers by allowing time for it every day. Allow for time in the day for students to read to the class.
Confidence Messages	Have all students write down a note with praise for another student and distribute them. (Keep the notes anonymous, if possible.)
Confident Reflections	Break students into small groups and allow them to share with each other about the books they are reading. Students can talk about the stories, then offer their opinions on them.

CLOSE READING LESSON

Bobby the Brave (Sometimes)

BY LISA YEE, ILLUSTRATED BY DAN SANTAT

Close reading is a thorough reading and rereading of text, making the process of reading visible. We demonstrate the reading process, illuminate fine writing techniques, and connect themes in support of the 7 Strengths Model.

Summary: *Bobby the Brave (Sometimes)* follows a boy who loves to skateboard, is a good friend, and shows confidence. Bobby has a stay-at-home father who was a professional linebacker, and his gym teacher expects Bobby to be good at football because his father was. Readers will love the funny moments and poignant lessons.

BEFORE READING

Discuss Confidence:

- What is something you're good at? How did you get good at it?
- How might confidence help you in school? At home?
- Can you name a time in your life when you felt confident about something? What were the conditions that made you feel that way?

Discuss the Book's Cover:

- Predict whether or not you think Bobby will show confidence during the story. What makes you think that?
- How could you describe Bobby just from looking at the cover?

DURING READING

As Bobby expected, Jillian, Jackson, and St. James picked the most athletic kids. When it was Bobby's turn to pick again, he called out, "Holly Harper."

A murmur ran through the class. A girl had never been on a team with the boys before. But the way Bobby figured it, since there were three boy team captains and one girl team captain, some girls would have to be with boys anyway. Holly high-fived with Chess as she took her place behind Bobby. When the last person was called, Bobby's team included Chess, Holly, Swoozie, Amy and Amelia (two girls Bobby always had trouble telling apart), and Kip, a boy who was semi-famous because in second grade he had broken both wrists in a freak bowling accident.

Interpretation:

- What might the author be revealing about Bobby's character when he was picking teams?
- What might be causing Bobby to choose his friends? Why might this show confidence?

you were doing push-ups, I heard you talking about me to Annie. You told her, 'He's not like me.' And then she said, 'That's for sure.'"

There. Bobby had said it. It felt good to have gotten it out, but rotten at the same time. He knew his father would never fire him, but when Mr. Ellis-Chan didn't say anything, Bobby worried that his dad might want to trade him to another team.

"Son," Mr. Ellis-Chan said gently. Bobby looked up. His father didn't look angry or disgusted; instead, he looked concerned. "What I was telling Annie was that I was proud of you. I could never skateboard as well as you. All those tricks you can do — they amaze me. I'm so big and clumsy on a skateboard. . . . I'm not like you."

Bobby was speechless. *That* was what his father meant?

Author's Craft:

- What does the author do to show the characters' inner thoughts?
- How does the author's use of dialogue help you understand Bobby's dilemma?

Interpretation:

- How did Bobby's confidence change how he acted?
- If you were in Bobby's situation, would you have done what he did or not? Why?

Standing up straight, Bobby said to Jillian Zarr, "I am not a disgrace. I am Bobby Ellis-Chan, and if you don't like that, then you can . . . you can . . . you can just go back to Mars!" And with that, Bobby turned on his heels and went to join the boys, as Jillian Zarr stood speechless.

AFTER READING

- How did Bobby show confidence in this story? What was your favorite example of Bobby's confidence?
- How did Bobby's confidence help him? What makes you think that?
- What kind of commitment can you make to building your own confidence?

▶ For other favorite books on confidence, see page 201.

Using Technology to Promote Confidence

- **Story sharing:** Have students use the free Scratch software from MIT (scratch.mit.edu) to create and share their own stories that deal with confidence.

- **Teleprompter:** Let students practice what they want to say during a class presentation.

- **Screencasts:** Have students create screencasts that show what they know about a topic.

- **Online journals:** Students use online journals to record reflections.

What You Can Do to Promote Confidence at Home

You can support families in continuing this work at home. They have a tremendous opportunity to create a warm and supportive culture that encourages children to take intellectual risks and to see themselves as having an important voice in the home and in the world. Confidence comes with perceived opportunities for success. The more kids feel that they are up for the challenge, the more confidence they will display.

Encourage families to give children ample time and space to practice confidence. Encourage family members to engage children often in conversation, asking them for their opinions of books they read and of current events. Give families confidence-building questions they can use that send the clear message to their children that their opinions matter.

- What do you think we should read tonight?

- How do you feel we should plan our homework schedule this week?

- How would you have handled that situation differently?

- I need your help. How might we solve this problem?

- How might you change the world?

Super Reader Family Guide

Actions to Develop Your Child's Sense of Confidence

I'm Proud of Me
Have all of the family members write down three reasons why they are proud of themselves.

Power Booster
Have all family members write down how they typically boost their confidence when they feel nervous or insecure. They do not have to share their Power Boosters, but they should use them in the future!

Constant Confidence
Build your child's confidence as a reader and speaker by allowing time for reading and speaking every day. For example, set time every day for family members to talk about what they are reading.

Confidence Notes
Have family members write anonymous notes of praise to one another.

Confident Reflections
Invite family members to talk about what they are reading. They can describe the texts first, then offer their opinions on them.

Routines to Develop Your Child's Sense of Confidence

- Give your child time to formulate opinions.

- Ask your child to share favorite books or stories during family gatherings.

- Encourage your child to speak up when participating in family conversations.

CHAPTER 8

STRENGTH 6: COURAGE

"I learned that courage was not the absence of fear, but the triumph over it."

—NELSON MANDELA

 For a video snapshot of courage in action, visit scholastic.com /superreaderresources.

Ernest is sitting in the hallway outside of the Tom Bradley room on the 26th floor of Los Angeles City Hall with a group of kids who will soon be addressing the mayor, members of the California State Senate, educational leaders, the news media, and 200 other guests. These students are part of a summer program in which kids conduct research to address social issues in their neighborhoods and communities. Each summer culminates with a public presentation of the work. As Ernest scans the students who are in various stages of preparation and rehearsal, he sees a mixture of anticipation, excitement, and genuine fear. He calls the students together and they begin to talk about why it is important to share their work. Some students comment that their research can change the way people think about kids. Others argue that they can change policies that affect their communities. Ernest responds that another important reason for them to share their work is that they will develop the courage to always speak their truth. Even in the face of fear, even in the face of overwhelming odds, those who have conviction and courage will know they can never be silenced. Daniel has been in many different foster care homes. When we read the Harry Potter books aloud to him, he says to us: "I love these books because while Harry has a scar on his forehead, I have one in my heart. But Harry and I, we are courageous."

Why Courage Matters

In the vignette, "In the LD (Learning Disabled) Bubble," Lynn Pelkey (2013) discusses her schooling experience as a child who began to expect to fail and saw her lack of ability as set. By middle school, Pelkey developed what she called a "learned helplessness." Several years later, her mother encouraged her to attend an open house at a community college and over time she learned, "I was not worthless, and my opinion mattered." Most importantly, she learned to become an advocate for herself. Her reading and writing abilities had not changed, but by sharing her needs with her professors, she received the type of modifications needed to ensure success. She learned to be courageous.

Whether a child is learning a new difficult skill or reimagining their ability to tackle a challenge, risk taking and courage play important roles. Risk taking begins with a decision to act, and courage provides the inspiration to act. According to Michael Agar (1994), being courageous rewards individuals from living a life of "being" to a life of "becoming." Courage is critical for change and growth to occur.

In her research on children learning to write, Anne Haas Dyson (1995) celebrates the teachers and children in a third-grade class who find the courage to take risks and become superheroes of writing. Students wrote themselves into the narratives they created. They defied stereotypes, became the main characters, and were powerful. One student, Tina, became a superhero in her story as she developed into a superhero writer. As Dyson notes, "Tina's writing took courage, for it was writing that was clearly rewriting—shifting the constructed world and the possibilities of the constructed self in notable ways." When children courageously begin to view themselves as superheroes of writing and reading, they transform from "being" to "becoming" and there are no limits to how far they can go and grow.

Becoming a super reader requires courage. Whether it is having the strength and perseverance required to tackle a difficult text or the will to act upon the things that we read that demand us to be different in the world, courage is key. Innovation and change come when courageous people act together to change the world. It was Nobel Prize-winning physicist Albert Einstein who said, "Any intelligent fool can make things bigger and more complex…it takes a touch of genius and a lot of courage to move in the opposite direction." As long as the world continually demands that we move in the opposite direction, we are going to need courageous women and men who are willing and able to act. We believe that our super readers will become these courageous geniuses!

What You Can Do to Promote Courage in School and in Out-of-School Programs

Use literature to activate a courageous spirit.

Books and stories, true and fictional, contemporary and historical, have extraordinary power to build worlds for children in which they can imagine themselves being courageous. They provide an example, yes, but also paint a picture of how a character or true-life person (or animal!) got to the point where he or she was able to do something breathtaking. However the courage comes, from going on one's first overnight to standing up to a bully to rescuing people in a dire situation, literature tells a child the story of the human heart and spirit.

Give children the opportunity to categorize books by types of courage in the classroom library. Invite them to name the types of courage they have seen and experienced and the kinds they have read about. Some types may include:

- courage to stand up for what you believe in
- courage to fight for a cause
- courage to do something no one has ever done
- courage to take a risk
- courage to create a new idea
- courage to challenge the way things have always been done

The children can make baskets for these courage types or files if they are reading online. They can use the baskets/files to meet with "courage partners" to talk about what types of courage most resonate with them as they read.

Whether they're learning about a kind of quiet courage from Bernard Waber's *Courage*, ways to overcome obstacles from Kobi Yamada's *What Do You Do With an Idea?*, or ways to make a creative mark from Peter Reynolds's *Ish*, super readers can discuss how real and fictional heroes take steps to become who they are by having courage.

You can share great biographies about people who exhibit courage in their daily lives and also by doing things that are truly breathtaking, such as *On a Beam of Light: A Story of Albert Einstein* by Jennifer Berne, *I Am Helen Keller* by Brad Meltzer, *The Man Who Walked Between the*

Towers by Mordicai Gerstein, and *Dave the Potter* by Laban Carrick Hill. The subjects of those books change the way we think about what "Yes I can!" means. They lead to rich discussion with children, especially if we keep the discussion open ended by asking questions such as the following:

- Where does courage come from?
- What made it grow inside these characters?
- How is it growing inside you?

Connect courage to the learning that happens across subject areas.

This is a strength that shows up in many different ways as children are reading across the school day—from social studies to science to all the ways they are learning about the world and the people in it. Help children identify ways different fields—from math to art to music to history—have made leaps and bounds because people were not afraid to speak up, to challenge ideas, and to come up with new ones.

Create book sets of biographies of people who achieved a lot in their lives alongside copies of the actual work they did. Pair great picture books such as *Viva Frida* by Yuyi Morales alongside prints of Frida Kahlo's art. Pair *Martin's Big Words* by Doreen Rappaport with video of Martin Luther King, Jr. giving speeches or printouts of his original speeches for students to read.

Find heroes everywhere and study them.

In the book *The Courage to Care*, the rescuers in the time of the Holocaust share their stories, and the beneficiaries of their courage share as well. Max Rothschild, a German survivor of the Holocaust who was aided in his escape from the Gestapo by the Dutch underground writes:

"In the fall of 1943, Niek Schouten, the one who saved my wife and me, dressed himself and a friend as Gestapo agents. They went on those bicycles with rubber wheels from house to house in a street in Rotterdam where Jews were living, and they said: 'We are from the Gestapo, and we have to pick up the children.' Then they put the children on the back of their bicycles and prepared to save them... In this way, they were able to save those children and many of us. Most of these rescuers consistently have refused to be honored. They cannot understand why they should be quoted, or cited, or given anything like a distinction of some kind or another. They want to forget about what they

did during the war, and just go on… living the way they have always lived. That is their great beauty."

Hermann Graebe saved the lives of more than 300 Jews in the Ukraine, Poland, and Germany. When asked why, he said:

"I cannot explain exactly why or how I did these things, but I believe my mother's influence on me when I was a child has a lot to do with it. My mother was a simple, uneducated person who came from a peasant family… and she told me, when I was 10 or 12 years old, that I should not take advantage of other people's vulnerability." (Rittner & Myers, 1989)

Of all the strengths in this book, courage is perhaps the rarest to experience on a daily basis, and yet once experienced, or even read about, it can be intensely transformational. Reading gives the child the window to a world in which people act with moral justice, and also a world in which people don't. The absence of courage in our world has caused grave pain and sorrow. Even our youngest readers, whether reading a simple book such as *The Mouse and the Lion,* where a mouse heroically helps a lion, or hearing a story of a grandmother who took heroic measures for her family, can grow into the kind of people we hope will lead our world, our future civic, professional, and community leaders, of whom courage is expected and nurtured. As Martin Luther King, Jr., once said, "The arc of the moral universe is long, but it bends toward justice."

Courageous Character Cards

By asking super readers to reflect on the actions and motives of brave characters in books, we encourage them to tap into the courage they need to overcome fears they have that may stand in the way of their learning.

Directions

1. **Introduce the lesson by saying:**

   Today we're going to do an activity to get us thinking about courage. Each of us will make a Courageous Character Card. But first, I'll give you time to think of a brave character from a book you've read and write it down.

2. **Once each student has chosen a character, have him or her write a list of moments the character was brave in the book. You can say:**

   Now that you have chosen a courageous character, take three minutes and write down a list of times that character showed that they were brave.

3. **Tell students they will now create their Courageous Character Cards. Distribute a sheet of unlined paper to each student, and ask him or her to hold it horizontally and fold it in half. Then, explain what will go on each side of the paper. You can say:**

   On the left side of the paper, you can draw a picture of your courageous character. You can draw them however you want: just the face, or you can draw them in action! On the right side, you can write about all the times they were brave. You can write this as a list, or you can jot down some short stories about the characters.

   Once you've drawn your characters and written about their courageous acts, feel free to decorate your Courageous Character Cards. (Offer markers, colored pencils, and any other supplies that will make for an exciting finished product.)

4. Invite students to share their Courageous Character Cards in pairs, small groups, or with the whole class. Lead a discussion about the activity by asking questions such as:

- Why did you choose this character?
- Did the character feel afraid at all before acting with courage? How do you know?
- If so, how do you think the character overcame his or her fear?

5. Connect the concept of courage to your reading community. Ask:

- What might someone in our reading community be afraid of? (List fears.)
- What are some good reasons to overcome these fears? (List reasons.)
- What are some things we can do to gain courage?
- How can we help others in our reading community gain courage?

Actions for Promoting Courage in School and in Out-of-School Programs

Courage Badges	Create creative badges for your child when he or she takes a new positive step as a reader.
Courage Time Line	Invite children to read about different historical figures and create a time line of courageous behaviors exhibited by these figures.
Reflections of Courage	Go around in a circle and invite children to discuss times they were courageous.
Books of Courage	Find examples of courage and life lessons in a book.
News Hour	Share stories based on current events and ask the students to identify specific acts of courage. Discuss ways they can be courageous in their own lives.

Just Juice

BY KAREN HESSE
ILLUSTRATED BY ROBERT ANDREW PARKER

Close reading is a thorough reading and rereading of text, making the process of reading visible. We demonstrate the reading process, illuminate fine writing techniques, and connect themes in support of the 7 Strengths Model.

Summary: *Just Juice* follows a girl named Juice, the middle child of five sisters. Juice doesn't like going to school because she has trouble reading. Instead, she spends time with her dad, who also struggles with reading, in his metal shop. *Just Juice* is a powerful story of overcoming obstacles.

BEFORE READING	**Discuss Courage:** • What does courage mean to you? • Who have you read about that has shown courage? • What is something you could do to show courage? **Discuss the Book's Cover:** • What might the girl's expression be revealing to us? • What do you wonder about the title of this book?
DURING READING	**Interpretation:** • What are you noticing about Juice's personality? • How might Juice's personality and nature be impacting her family?

> I don't want Pa to feel bad. I want to make him happy. I want to tell him I won't love him any less if I can read. Pa and me, we've been careful, tiptoeing around this particular secret. But I can't let Pa's half of the secret keep me from doing something about mine.

Author's Craft:

- Why do you think the author chose to have white space in this section? What might that be showing?

> "No, thank you, ma'am," Officer Rusk says to Ma's offering the bowl of sugar.
>
> He looks sad at being here. Real sad. I feel sorry for him.
>
> "I'll come to school," I say.
>
> Officer Rusk looks at me.
>
> "I'll come. Tomorrow. Tell Miss Hamble I'll be there."

Interpretation:

- Why might this be hard for Juice?
- What do you think the author is showing us about Juice's personality?

> I look once more. Zero three zero. I just have to be right.
>
> "How do I bring up your sugar, Ma?" I ask.
>
> Her eyes are staring up at the ceiling. I can tell she isn't hearing me.
>
> My hands are shaking as I push a chair over to the shelves and climb up and dig behind the cracker box and the noodles until I find the sugar cubes.

AFTER READING

- What might you learn from Juice about how she practices courage?
- What is an action step you could take to practice courage in your life?

▶ For other favorite books on courage, see page 202.

What You Can Do to Promote Courage at Home

Families have an important and unique role to play in building courage at home. You can support families by encouraging specific literacy-based activities that encourage the building of courage.

Help families select books that address themes of courage by sending home samples from the list on page 202. Encourage families to have conversations about the big ideas in the books. Send home conversation starters such as:

- What is your personal definition of courage?

- Where have you all seen examples of quiet courage in our community?

- Where have we experienced or witnessed courage in our family?

Invite families to develop a family definition of courage, and talk about how that definition might be the same or different from the way courage is portrayed in popular media. Have families make "Courage Goals" and hang them somewhere for the rest of the family to admire. Remind families to note and celebrate moments when members of the family demonstrated courage. Have families share "courage" stories from their own cultures and prior experiences. Post those stories on a class blog.

Super Reader Family Guide

Actions to Develop Your Child's Sense of Courage

Courage Badges

Create a badge for your child when he or she takes a new positive step as a reader.

Courage Time Line

Invite your child to read about different historical figures and create a time line of courageous behaviors he or she sees in those figures.

News Hour

As a family, watch the news and identify acts of courage you hear about. Discuss ways your child can be courageous in life.

Reflections of Courage

Have a family discussion about times each family member was courageous.

Books of Courage

Find examples of courage and life lessons in a book.

Routines to Develop Your Child's Sense of Courage

- Support your child when he or she stands up for a big idea and/or a friend.

- Point out examples of strong leadership in real life and in the books your child reads.

- Commend your child when taking risks with reading new material. Let him or her know that it requires tremendous courage to become a super reader.

- Share and discuss a story about a time in your life when you took a risk and needed to show courage.

- Give your child the opportunity to show courage by encouraging a new activity, such as a sport or dance.

- Celebrate moments of success and reflect on moments of failure as positive steps in growing. When discussing the meaning of success, focus more on courage and effort than on outcomes.

- Have your child act out his or her writing or someone else's writing that speaks to a sense of courage.

CHAPTER 9

STRENGTH 7: HOPE

"I believe in one day and someday
and this perfect moment called Now."

—JACQUELINE WOODSON, from *Brown Girl Dreaming*

A group of young adolescents are having a class discussion. Ms. Garcia, their teacher, has asked them to define a critical poem. One student offers that a critical poem is about changing the world. Ms. Garcia asks, "How does a critical poem change the world?" Another student comments that critical poems point to problems, but they also point to solutions to problems we face in society. Several students chime in making similar points about how critical poets go "deeper," and how they deal with serious issues in their poems. Sandra is a relatively new student in the class. She has been kicked out of her previous school and her attendance to date has been sporadic. Up to this point, she hasn't added anything to the conversation, but she quickly shifts her body in a way that commands the attention of the class as she exclaims in desperation, "How can a poem change the world! I mean, can a poem really change the world?" The class is quiet and thoughtful and a young woman sitting near Sandra responds, "What if that poem changes the poet, and then that poet changes the world? Then the poem changes the world, because it changes the poet." Sandra looks her classmate in the eye and she is almost in tears. She whispers almost inaudibly, "Nice. I like that. The poet changes the world."

For a video snapshot of hope in action, visit scholastic.com /superreaderresources.

Moses is 10 years old. He came to New York City from Guyana the year before. The very first sentence he writes in his life is his memoir: "I was the lonely deaf." This memoir explained to the class how isolated his life was back home and how excited he is to be part of the community of new friends who understand him and who understand his loneliness. Moses loves science books, anything about the way the body works, and books about animals and nature. He browses and studies them carefully. Later in the year, he writes: "My name is Moses. I will become a doctor. I will take care of people." Moses, finding a home with others, reading his way to a deep understanding of his passions and his own strengths, writes from a place of strength: a world of hope.

Why Hope Matters

Hope is a basic human need. When we lose our hope, we lose our humanity. For more than two decades, Shawn Ginwright has worked with students who have experienced tremendous suffering in their lives. The difference, he argues, between the kids who are able to confront and ultimately overcome obstacles and those who are unsuccessful, is hope. To that end, he now makes teaching kids to hope the focus of his work with educators. His book *Hope and Healing in Urban Education: How Urban Activists and Teachers Are*

Reclaiming Matters of the Heart (2015) profiles successful educators and community leaders who are using reading and writing to instill hope in communities. Ginwright's message is powerful. Hope not only makes the difference, hope is the difference. When we instill hope in children, we help them to understand that they are powerful readers and thinkers and speakers and doers with so much to share with the world. When we help them to see that dynamic and thoughtful people change the world on a daily basis, we not only create super readers, but also change the world.

What You Can Do to Promote Hope in School and in Out-of-School Programs

Use literature to promote hope.

The poet Emily Dickinson wrote that hope was "the thing with feathers," and that is really what literature does for children: it gives them feathers to fly. The super reader is soaring over the difficulties of the day, thanks to the comfort that a wonderful story, an uplifting poem, or a funny comic brings. The super reader is visiting worlds where many hopeful things are possible. The thing with feathers is the book—the words on the page that send the super reader flying.

However, of all the strengths, hope can be the most abstract, the most elusive. Literature shows us the way. Consider organizing your classroom library around the ways we think about hope—or for what we typically hope:

- ourselves
- our families
- our community
- our world

All the texts we read with children can be framed around these lenses: self, family, community, and world. Invite children to look through those lenses when discussing a read aloud, when working on their independent reading, and when working or talking in small groups or with partners.

Create a hope read-aloud collection. Let children know that when super readers get discouraged in life, they often turn to cherished texts that lift them up and inspire them. Poems such as "My People" by Langston Hughes, picture books such as *Owen and Mzee* and *Beekle*, chapter books such as *Because of Winn-Dixie*; *Bud, Not Buddy*; and *The Crossover* can offer children a springboard to talk about times when hope prevails over sorrow or adversity.

Have goal-driven, outcome-driven, affirmational expectations.

Hope is about celebration. There are times when we are working in places where life is extremely difficult for children—places where it seems there is no opportunity to experience the joy of hope at all. But children will always find a way. They crave hope, they want hope, they need hope to thrive. In order for them to have hope, we have to practice it with them every day. And it is not only children experiencing deprivation who need this.

Hope is about feeling unique, necessary, and valued in the world, and how we translate that feeling to action and forward motion. Here are some ways to do that across the day with super readers:

- Set a self-, community, or world goal at the start of each week. Check in on that goal at the end of the week.

- Have a mini-celebration (with food if possible!) to share how the goal is progressing.

- Tap into how super reading is impacting those goals. If a self-goal is: "I am going to be a better brother to my baby sister," what kinds of books can that reader collect and read in and out of school to foster that hope coming true?

- Keep a basket of Hope Stars. Add the stars to the walls of the classroom when you see a goal being accomplished that represents the larger hopes and dreams of your classroom community.

Help children dream big.

Every kid deserves the chance to dream big. We can practice this with children from the very youngest ages. Dreaming big means making plans so hope feels purposeful, disciplined, and intentional. For super readers of all ages, use graphic organizers that help them plan dreams.

If a child's dream is to become a doctor, have some of her reading and writing work be around that idea, and say to her, "I believe in this dream of yours. I want to help you think about it." Then, create reading baskets or online folders with ways for children to read about their dreams and to make lists, organize ideas, and interview people about their hopes. Maybe they want to start a lemonade stand. Maybe they want to invent something new. Maybe they do want to become a doctor. Whatever that dream is, honor it, revel in it, and make super reading a part of it.

Another idea is to create dream catchers to hang in the classroom that show one big dream every child has. Give children a chance to change what's in the dream catcher at least four times a year.

HOPE FOCUS LESSON

Hope Heart Maps

By having super readers create Hope Heart Maps, you can forge a strong connection between hope, goal setting, and reading.

Directions

1. **Introduce the lesson by saying:**

   We are making Hope Heart Maps today. To make our Hope Heart Maps, we are all going to think about all of the things we are hopeful about.

2. **Begin by asking each student to turn to a clean sheet of paper. You can say:**

   Along the top of your paper, write the phrase "I am hopeful about." (Show an example.) Once you've all written this, I'm going to give you three minutes to answer the question, what are you hopeful about? Each of us will make a list of our hopes. Keep in mind, our hopes can be a lot of things! Maybe it's a certain date like your birthday, or maybe it's a goal of yours like being able to finish a chapter book. There are no wrong answers!

3. **After students have made their lists, ask them to turn their papers over and draw a heart as big as they can. (The page can be horizontal or vertical.)**

4. **Ask students to write the different hopes they have inside their hearts. Ask students to include hopes that they want to come true soon, as well as hopes for the future when they're grown up. Be sure some of their hopes relate to reading.**

5. **If time and resources allow, invite students to decorate their Hope Heart Maps.**

6. **Be sure to leave a few minutes for sharing work and discussing the activity. Praise everyone for his or her creativity and willingness to explore and share hopes. Suggestions for guiding questions include:**

   - Which hopes are most important to you?
   - What is one way you can help one of your hopes come true?
   - Which of your hopes can come true by being a strong reader? Explain.

7. **Display the Hope Heart Maps in your classroom.**

8. As an extension activity, invite family members to come together and discuss the words they put in their hearts and the positive changes they would like to see and make in the world.

Actions for Promoting Hope in School and in Out-of-School Programs

Group Goals	Have the class come together and set goals for themselves. Suggestions include:
	    Reading independently for a certain amount of time out of school
	    Creating a book club

Admire Hope	Invite students to choose a hopeful character from a book they have read, and write about how they can learn from him or her.
I Have Hope	Have students create specific personal reading goals, such as, "I want to read four new genres this marking period." and "I want to read for 15 minutes straight without getting distracted." Occasionally check in with students on their goals and help them set new ones.
Hope Wall	Invite students to think of something that they are hopeful about. Then, have them choose an image to represent it. Have all of the students add their images to one poster that you put up in the classroom.
Stories of Hope	Have students listen to a speech, poem, or other presentation that you feel embodies hope. Lead a discussion about how the speech made them feel, and any lessons they can take from the speaker.

March On! The Day My Brother Martin Changed the World

BY CHRISTINE KING FARRIS
ILLUSTRATED BY LONDON LADD

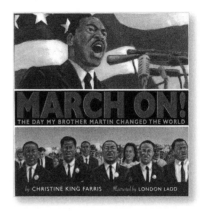

Close reading is a thorough reading and rereading of text, making the process of reading visible. We demonstrate the reading process, illuminate fine writing techniques, and connect themes in support of the 7 Strengths Model.

Summary: Written by Dr. Martin Luther King, Jr.'s sister, Christine King Farris, *March On!* details the day leading up to Dr. King's famous "I Have Dream" speech. The book recounts images of those who marched to Washington, D.C. on that monumental day in civil rights history. The wording clearly evokes the hope of all the marchers and of Dr. King that some day the world will change.

BEFORE READING

Discuss Hope:

- What does the word *hope* mean to you?
- When you think of hope, what other words come to mind?
- What are you hopeful for about the future?

Discuss the Book's Cover:

- What do the colors and portraits tell you about possible themes?
- Consider the title. Let's discuss it in the context of hope.

DURING READING

Author's Craft:

- Why might the author have chosen to repeat words? What emphasis is the author trying to convey?
- Why might the author have capitalized the last line?

Peace is certainly what Martin had on his mind as he stood next to the marble statue of President Abraham Lincoln, where he spent most of the afternoon helping other speakers put the final touches on their speeches, and shaking hands with people who had come, too, to make their voices heard.

Interpretation:

- What themes might the author be conveying through the demonstrators' actions? What role might hope be playing in these scenes?

My brother Martin had a dream. He shared it with the marchers. He shared it with the nation. And the world. It was a beautiful, inspirational dream. One day, he said, children would live in a nation where they would be judged by the content of their character, not the color of their skin—where black boys and girls would be able to join hands with white boys and girls as sisters and brothers.

Interpretation:

- What feelings do you think Martin was trying to stir in his audience?
- How do you think Martin's words made his audience feel more hopeful?

AFTER READING

- In what way does the strength of hope inform the entire book?
- Let's discuss Martin's message. What kind of hope do you believe the author feels it gave the world? What do you think?
- What are your greatest hopes for yourself, your community, and your world?

▶ For other favorite books on hope, see page 203.

Using Technology to Promote Hope

- **Scratch:** Have students use the free Scratch software from MIT (scratch.mit.edu) to create their own video games that inspire hope.

- **PicCollage:** Students create goal posters to chart their progress as they pursue one of their goals.

- **Toontastic:** Make a movie that shows how students are becoming lifelong learners.

- **Facebook:** Share pictures of lifelong reading behaviors on social media.

What You Can Do to Promote Hope at Home

Encourage families to nurture the dreams and aspirations of their children. Remind families that reactions to their children's ideas and attitudes can mean the difference between a hopeful student and a disengaged student. Provide examples of ways families can support the positive spirit of a child at home.

- When students face challenges, families can encourage hope and resilience and a belief that any challenge can be met by affirming the small steps the child took and telling stories of one's own life to help the child envision a hopeful future.

- Make a notebook together or put a list on the refrigerator of a family "hope of the week."

Encourage families to nurture a sense of hope by bringing books into the home that focus on hope. For a complete list of books, see page 203. Suggest conversation starters to get discussions going at home that instill a hopeful point of view in children:

- Who makes you feel hopeful? Why?

- What hopes do you have for the future?

- What do you hope will happen today? Tomorrow? This year?

- How can you help someone else feel hopeful?

Encourage families to seek out models of hope and inspiration. Families can point to people in their family, in the community, and in their cultural history who stood for hope. Ask families to share biographies of great leaders like Harriet Tubman or Cesar Chavez who stood for hope and change. Families can include hopeful sayings in the home, as well, from people like Toni Morrison or Mahatma Gandhi that speak to hope and being the change we'd like to see in the world.

Super Reader Family Guide

Actions to Develop Your Child's Sense of Hope

Family Goals

As a family, set a goal for yourselves:

- Read a book together.
- Do a family activity.
- Have dinner together every night for a week.
- Do something to help the community.

Embody Hope

Invite family members to choose a hopeful character from a book, and write about how they can learn from him or her.

I Have Hope

Develop a sense of hope after reading stories with characters who persevere through challenges. Talk about what hope means and why it's important to the lives of the characters.

Hope Wall

Invite family members to think of something that they are hopeful about. Then, have them choose an image to represent it. Add the images to a poster that you put up in the home.

Stories of Hope

Invite your family to come together and listen to a speech, poem, or other presentation that you feel embodies hope. Lead a discussion about how the speech made your family feel, and any lessons they can take from the speaker.

Routines to Develop Your Child's Sense of Hope

- Make a wish for the community, country, or world and share it with someone who is in a place that is meaningful to your child.

- Find stories in the world about hope and optimism (on social media, in the newspaper, in what you read together). Ask your child to make connections.

- Have conversations on goal setting for a variety of purposes: playing sports, learning at school, socializing with friends, engaging in civic activities.

- Talk to your child about his or her hopes, set one concrete goal, and help your child work toward the goal.

- Create a family story book (in photos, pictures, and/or words) that focuses on hope-driven ideas.

- Ask your child to point out conflicts and resolutions in the books he or she is reading. What is the life lesson? How does the character overcome his or her challenges?

- Have your child express in writing his or her hopes for the community or for the world. Send his or her finished piece to local community organizations.

- Ask your local librarian to create a list of books in which characters maintain hope in challenging situations.

Next Steps in the Journey

Now that you've had an opportunity to visit each strength up close, it's time to turn to Part II, which looks at the 7 Strengths Model in action. This section is full of best practices, strategies for independent reading, management techniques, and planning and assessment tools, all designed to help you promote super reading in classrooms, in out-of-school programs, and at home.

THE 7 STRENGTHS MODEL IN ACTION

Super Reading in School, in Out-of-School Programs, and at Home

CHAPTER 10

BEST PRACTICES FOR SUPER READERS

"Once you learn to read, you will be forever free."

–FREDERICK DOUGLASS

The belief that students who feel emotionally secure, supported, and connected to learning will be better prepared to achieve academically is a foundational tenet of the 7 Strengths Model. The classroom culture, discourse, and even physical set-up all play key roles in fostering this type of support and engagement. In this chapter, we will discuss best practice teaching methods that strengthen all readers and how to implement them in your classroom.

Teaching Methods That Strengthen Super Readers

Successful reading instruction incorporates a gradual release of responsibility from the teacher to the student. Effective teachers model what successful, engaged readers do, but they also allow students extended time to apply and practice what they have learned about reading. Teaching structures, such as the read aloud and small-group work, teach children all the rules and tricks of super reading, and then the independent practice lets them *play the game.*

No matter your setting, you can create an accordion flow to your classroom management that creates opportunities for explicit instruction as well as independent practice. The following table describes the teaching model we call "whole-small-whole."

Whole-Small-Whole Teaching Sequence	
Whole	The teacher gathers the entire class and uses high-quality literature to model a skill or strategy and to build reading community values.
Small	The teacher breaks the class into small groups, pairs, or individuals. The students apply and practice what they learned in the whole-group lesson, usually in the context of independent reading. The teacher coaches students in their efforts and uses this time to address the needs of individuals through conferences or small-group instruction.
Whole	The teacher gathers the entire class. Students share results of the independent work, reflect on how it went, and articulate why it was helpful to them as readers.

Read Aloud

What Is It? An "expert" reading of an authentic text chosen from a variety of genres and levels to an audience of one or more.

Why Is Reading Aloud Helpful to Super Readers? One of the most beneficial activities to nurture a super reader is the simple act of reading text aloud to children. We distinguish two kinds of read alouds, one in which we stop and "teach into" the text, and another that is meant to be more "immersive." We recommend at least one instructional read aloud a day and two ritual read alouds a day in a six-hour school day and at least one of each in an after-school session (for all ages). The read alouds should come from a variety of genres, and a read aloud can be short (a poem!) or longer (a chapter or an article or blog post). Texts can be used in either of these structures, and the same text can be used instructionally at one point in the day and then revisited for pure enjoyment later in the day.

Instructional Read Aloud	Ritual Read Aloud
• Offers opportunity for instruction in genre, strategy, and comprehension • Cultivates vocabulary development • Builds understanding and comprehension in texts	• Fosters a love of reading and models the processes of reading (stamina, enjoyment, engagement) • Fills the ear with the richness of literary and informational texts • Introduces texts, genres, and authors to students

Reading aloud to young children stimulates the growth of the essential cognitive functions that lead to literacy development, such as narrative and informational text comprehension and visual imagery (Duke & Martin, 2015). Researchers have actually discovered that babies who were read Dr. Seuss before birth recognized the same text after they were born (DeCasper & Spence, 1986).

A recent study used functional magnetic resonance imaging to show how children's brains develop in relation to how much they had been read to at home. Children with more exposure to read alouds had significantly greater activation in the areas of the brain responsible for visualization and multisensory integration (Hutton, Horowitz-Kraus, Mendelsohn, Dewitt, & Holland, 2015). Unfortunately, research also shows that many families stop reading to their children once they begin to do it on their own, yet the benefits of the family read aloud can continue indefinitely (Trelease, 2006). After all, even as adults, many of us enjoy books on tape or listening to authors read their own words.

Reading aloud is a profoundly essential activity for reading success, particularly for emergent readers (Fisher, Flood, Lapp, & Frey, 2004). In 1985, the government report, *Becoming a Nation of Readers* (Anderson, Hiebert, Scott, & Wilkinson) stated that "the single most important activity for building the knowledge required for eventual success in reading is reading aloud to children" (p. 23) and current research continues to support this finding (Lesesne, 2006). Children of all ages should be given the opportunity to participate daily in this high-joy, high-impact activity, at home and in classroom settings.

The read aloud is how we make the work of reading "visible." Reading aloud is a skill and art, especially when we are sharing with children (Braxton, 2007). While there are specific suggestions for making a read aloud as engaging and enjoyable as possible, such as introducing a story and building background knowledge, the most important way to excite children about reading and a particular text is to let inhibitions go, reread as needed, and be as expressive as possible. Ultimately, as librarian and author Barbara Braxton suggests, "Reading aloud is such a simple pleasure, but it can be a complex task. If you enjoy yourself, however, the children will, too."

Families whose primary home language differs from the school language should be encouraged to read aloud in the language with which they are most comfortable. Skills, strategies, and a passion for reading can be taught in any language and research has consistently shown that "development of children's home language supports their learning of English" (Wiley & de Klerk, 2010, p. 403). Families can be supported in locating printed and digital multimedia texts in their home language and encouraged to help their children grow as super readers in multiple languages.

The stunning fact of the research is this: children who are read aloud to on a daily basis consistently outperform their peers, reaching levels almost a year ahead of children who are not read aloud to (Kalb & van Ours, 2013). In the classroom, when students actively listen to a read aloud rather than participate round robin style, they benefit from the teacher's modeling of fluency and the immediate engagement of hearing a wonderful story told well. Not only are children expanding their oral vocabularies, they are learning new concepts in a pleasurable way (Blachowicz & Fisher, 2015). The read aloud invites children to sink into the world of a book and to flex the muscles of their imaginations as the story plays out in their minds.

The 7 Strengths and Read Aloud

- Bring the 7 Strengths to the forefront by reading aloud books that connect to each strength.

- Recognize when the 7 Strengths emerge as central ideas in your read alouds.

- Acknowledge how reading aloud together brings us closer as a community and fosters a sense of belonging.

- Encourage students to express curiosity about the content of texts by asking questions about the content and illustrations and making and confirming predictions.

- Satisfy students' curiosity by prompting them to research and read aloud the answers to the class to their many questions about the world as they come up.

- Help students build courage to read aloud with fluency and expression in front of others.

- Have students turn and talk about their hopes and dreams before, during, and after the read aloud.

Close Reading

What Is It? Reading at increasing levels of comprehension, from basic understanding of the text's message to understanding its structure, craft, and style to understanding its purpose and theme.

Why Is Close Reading Helpful to Super Readers? Super readers are close and critical readers. They read carefully and thoughtfully, asking critical questions of the texts they read. It is powerful to create the contexts in which children become close and critical readers. For example, Ernest sometimes has his students participate in mock trials and debates based on the literature they read. Because they know that they will be responsible for all of the material covered in the book, they generally read it more carefully. Also, when students are reading as part of research for a report that they are going to share with an audience, they tend to pay close attention to detail.

Close reading gives you the chance to linger over text with your students to allow for deeper and more analytical understandings of key pieces of literature and informational text. You get the chance to model *what, how*, and *why* we read. Immersing your students in close reading gives them the opportunity to learn the "look" and "feel" of language, to practice code breaking and meaning making together, to see the process of reading made visible. Students become strong, bold readers, approaching even the most difficult texts with new confidence in their abilities to decode what an author is trying to convey.

Close reading can happen during whole-class instruction, small-group lessons, and conferences with individual students. Deep analysis should be done with complex texts, therefore close readings need to be very scaffolded (and work best in small-group or one-on-one conferences).

General Close Reading Protocol for All Grades and Genres	
Preview	Examine the overall form and features of the text.
Read for what the text says	Try to summarize what the text is mainly about. Clarify unknown words.
Read for how the text is written	Analyze the author's choices of structure, words, and phrases to deepen your understanding of the text.
Read for why the text is written	Determine purpose and central ideas of the text.

Examining author's craft is a crucial part of close reading. Our students studied why Ezra Jack Keats decided to make the boy's coat red in *The Snowy Day*, and why he never named his character. One child said: "I believe Mr. Keats used only pronouns because he wanted us to feel like we could be the boy." Another child said: "I am a close reader of the footprints in the snow. Are they going forward or away? Maybe Mr. Keats wanted us to wonder." A third said: "I love how he used white space. It was like the snow itself, so quiet on that winter's day."

Encourage students to use text evidence to support any claims or conclusions they have about a text. See chart on the next page.

Explaining Thinking Using Text Evidence

Phrases to scaffold readers when they share their thinking orally and in writing:

- I think this because _____.
- The author shows this on page ___ where it says _____.
- There is proof of my thinking on page _____.
- There is evidence of this on page ___ where it states that _____.
- In the _____ (e.g., text, photo, article, letter, chart, cartoon, graph, speech, etc.), the author/artist states/shows _____.
- This idea is supported by the _____ (e.g., text, photo, article, letter, chart, cartoon, graph, speech, etc.). [Explain how.]
- An example from the _____ (e.g., text, photo, article, letter, chart, cartoon, graph, speech) is _____.

Other phrases to cite evidence:

- This clearly proves that _____.
- It is obvious that _____.
- Clearly, _____.
- It is evident that _____.
- This demonstrates _____.
- This makes it clear that _____.

Other useful verbs for explaining why a source supports your ideas include: *shows, conveys, justifies, supports, exemplifies, suggests, illustrates, displays.*

The 7 Strengths and Close Reading

- Encourage students to be curious about the choices authors make. Word choice, character development, plot development, illustration details, and more are thoughtfully included to impact the meaning of a text. Super readers notice these elements when they read closely and consider why authors shape them the way they do.

- Have students do close reading partnerships or small groups where reading friends can help each other by collaborating on ideas.

- Help students build the confidence to do the hard work of comprehending challenging text.

- Insist on kindness toward all readers in the class regardless of skill level. Students will engage in close reading and all reading activities with varying levels of success. We are all growing as readers alongside each other.

Small-Group Instruction

What Is It? A meeting with two or more students in which the teacher helps them achieve common learning goals as readers.

Why Is Small-Group Instruction Helpful to Super Readers? The most effective small-group instruction occurs when a teacher starts with formal or informal data to match students with similar needs together. He then convenes a manageable group of two to seven students to engage them in a lesson focused on a skill or strategy that they need. Meeting with small groups allows teachers to differentiate instruction effectively and efficiently. Students get more direct attention from the teacher than during whole-class instruction, and the teacher has the opportunity to choose texts and teaching objectives that closely address the needs of the group members. In small groups, students benefit from hearing the questions and ideas of fellow group members and solving challenges with and for each other.

The 7 Strengths and Small-Group Instruction

- Encourage students to be supportive reading friends by showing kindness to each other at all times and compassion for each other's challenges. Actively provide coaching for students as they practice sharing their conclusions and views with confidence. Encourage them to support their ideas with text evidence whenever possible.

- Urge students to work through mistakes in small-group reading. Students should treat each other's mistakes with kindness and be able to make mistakes without losing their confidence.

- Help students recognize that working in small groups often allows them to build the courage they need to be successful as independent readers. Recognize their growth and teach toward independence.

Collaborating With Peers: Reading Partners

What Is It? A meeting of two students reading and discussing their reading together.

Why Are Reading Partners Helpful to Super Readers? The super reader loves to talk about her reading. And she is listening, too. The partnership structure, even two times a week, is a valuable way for children to practice speaking and listening to each other about books. These partnerships can be flexible, changing each week or each month. They can be partnerships based on the following:

- interests
- favorite authors
- similar reading level
- similar reading challenge
- similar reading goal
- primary language
- project-based learning

Reading partners may happen in a variety of contexts: as quick meet-ups at any point in the day to check in on each other's reading or share something read outside of the classroom, during whole-class instruction as a Turn and Talk, or during small-group instruction or independent reading. This is a highly flexible structure that should come to feel natural for the children so they can feel supported by a partner whether or not they are reading the same book. Scaffold students conversation by providing and role-playing with conversation stems such as those in the chart that follows.

Crafting Longer and Stronger Conversations	
Describe	I noticed that… I see that… I hear you saying…
React	I agree/disagree because… This makes me feel _____ because… I think _____ because… That's amazing/cool/funny… This reminds me of…
Question	I am wondering… Why did the (author, poet, creator, photographer, illustrator)…? Why is…? Why does…?
Evaluate	I like how… I do not like how… My favorite thing is… I really enjoyed… The most important thing is…
Clarify	What did you mean? Can you explain? I feel confused about… I don't understand…
Draw Conclusions	This gives me a clue that… I think that the message is… This teaches a lesson about…
Speculate	I think that maybe… I am guessing that…
Expand	What do you think? Tell me more about that. Let me add to what _____ just said… That's true… plus… I also (noticed, thought, wondered)…

You can strengthen partnerships using the 7 Strengths by encouraging these behaviors in students:

Belonging: I greet my partner and give a compliment.

Curiosity: I ask questions about things my partner has to say.

Friendship: I show a connection when talking to my partner.

Kindness: I listen to what my partner has to say.

Confidence: I provide constructive feedback.

Courage: I work with different people in my class—even if they're not my best friends.

Hope: I set reading goals with my partner.

Collaborating With Peers: Reading Clubs

What Is It? Small groups of students reading a common text and engaging in discussion about it.

Why Are Reading Clubs Helpful to Super Readers? This is a fun way for your students to have longer sustained conversations and to get to know each other as readers. The club should, like partnerships, have a start and end date and the same children should not be expected to stay together in one club all year. It is to mix the levels of the children so they can experience different kinds of conversation. For example, a club could meet for a week to talk about poetry, or the club could meet for two weeks to talk about the theme of bullying. In these two cases, the club does not have to commit to reading the same text at the same time. When the same text will be read, it may make more sense to match children by their reading levels.

There should also be time for children to talk to one another about what they are reading and writing. Talk should also be initiated by students and geared toward their interests and curiosities. In her book *Classroom Discourse: The Language of Teaching and Learning*, Courtney Cazden (1988) identified that most classroom talk was initiated by and directed toward the teacher. Similarly, Gordon Wells (1989) found that lower-income and ethnolinguistic minority students had the fewest opportunities to initiate and participate in classroom talk. He calls for more talk that is 1) student owned, 2) inquiry driven, and 3) integrated with thinking, doing, reading, and writing. To prepare our children for the communicative world of the 21st century, they will need to become better speakers and listeners. This is facilitated by offering multiple opportunities for them to interact with one another.

The 7 Strengths and Collaborating With Peers

- Develop a sense of belonging by helping students find peers to talk with about reading.

- Help students develop friendships in ways that relate directly to academics.

- Build students' confidence and courage by making sure their peers are supportive and active companions in the reading experience.

- Spread hope by letting students know they are trusted members of the community and that their engagement with a particular text, type of text, or idea is truly valued and heard.

Creating an Environment That Supports and Engages Super Readers

Increasing reading engagement is essential to increasing literacy achievement and developing lifelong readers. Super readers by definition are engaged readers. In order to raise a super reader, we must find strategies to promote engagement.

In his 2004 *Journal of Literacy Research* article, John Guthrie describes a study of third graders and their literacy engagement. He found that 9-year-olds whose family background was characterized by low income and low education, but who were highly engaged readers, substantially outscored students who came from backgrounds with higher education and income, but who themselves were less engaged readers. Guthrie also found that engaged readers spend up to 500 percent more time reading than disengaged readers. He encourages families and teachers to increase reading time by 200–500 percent and to foster engagement through conceptual themes, hands-on experiences, self-directed learning, interesting texts, classroom discourse, and time for extended reading.

The following practices are designed to foster a classroom culture that celebrates reading and helps to create a classroom environment that nurtures the growth of super readers.

How We Use the 7 Strengths

Strength	What we do as super readers...
BELONGING	We work together to create a learning community that explores the world and all kinds of literature.
CURIOSITY	We feed our curious minds by asking and answering questions about what we read.
FRIENDSHIP	We bond because of our shared passions. We build identities as readers by working together.
KINDNESS	We support one another, working together to reach new heights as readers.
CONFIDENCE	We practice reading every day, using new strategies and skills to help us become fearless and strong.
COURAGE	We understand that reading can be challenging and aren't afraid to work through the hard parts.
HOPE	We set goals for ourselves as readers and use those goals to think about the future.

Identity Building

What Is It? Instruction aimed at building students' awareness of their preferences, habits, strengths, and challenges as readers.

Why Is Identity Building Helpful to Super Readers? First and foremost, we strive to help all of our students recognize themselves as readers, regardless of age, skill level, language proficiency, or any other classifications that cause students to consider themselves outsiders from the group that calls themselves "readers." There is no pivotal moment when one becomes a reader. An infant listening to a story read aloud is just as much of a reader as a scientist reading a professional journal. We are all on different places in our unique reading journeys. As educators and parents, we must assure all children that they, too, are readers. This is the first step of creating a reading identity. Once that critical foundation is established, we can help readers build on it by helping them identify other important aspects of their reading identity:

- What do you like to read about?

- Who is a favorite author?

- Where do you like to read?

- What is easy for you as a reader?

- What is challenging for you as a reader?

- What goals do you need to work on to become stronger as a reader?

- What kinds of books do you like to read?

- What genres would you like to explore next?

Super readers have answers to these types of questions, and the answers will evolve over time as they continue to learn and grow.

The 7 Strengths and Identity Building

- Assure students that all children in the classroom are readers and belong to the classroom reading community.

- Help students develop curiosity about authors, genres, and books through engaging library displays, book talks, and peer recommendations.

- Provide frequent opportunities for students to share their reading preferences and make recommendations with confidence to their reading friends in the group.

- Satisfy students' hopes to grow as readers by helping them set goals and monitoring progress toward them.

Reading Celebrations

What Is It? Recognition of achievements, both small and large, of each student in the classroom.

Why Are Reading Celebrations Helpful to Super Readers? Every day, be sure to find something you admire in your children as readers. The goal is that by the end of the week, each child will have heard at least one specific thing about his or her growth as a reader. Be as specific as you can. "Bobby, I so loved how you worked with your partner." "Sarah, I really liked how you got comfortable quickly in your reading spot this week."

Celebrate your children as readers by honoring each small step. "I appreciate how you read in a one-inch voice so that others could read quietly." "I liked how you reread that passage when you didn't understand." Don't let anything small escape your attention. These are teachable moments.

Have weekly reading celebrations. Use the opportunity to have children read to a guest or have a guest reader join the class for the day. Let the weekly celebrations celebrate small steps: that a read aloud had longer discussion, or a child felt that she read for more minutes. Have children share out their gains in these ways. Some of the ways you can celebrate include:

Stamina: We read for more minutes this week.

Volume: We read many words this week.

Engagement: We were focused on our reading this week.

Comprehension: We had great book talks this week.

Identity: We changed and grew as readers this week.

Collaboration: We worked well with our partners this week.

The 7 Strengths and Reading Celebrations

- Recognize students' accomplishments, even their smallest accomplishments, to develop a sense of belonging.

- Cultivate a culture of affirmation, build a spirit of kindness for all.

- Deepen friendship by encouraging students to interact and engage with peers as readers (not only as playmates).

- Inspire hope by creating an atmosphere of enjoyment and pleasure around the reading experience.

The Classroom Library

What Is It? A large collection of texts (e.g., books, magazines, digital texts, pictures) available to students in a classroom.

Why Are Classroom Libraries Helpful to Super Readers? A classroom library provides super readers with the most critical tool we can give them—texts to read. Readers thrive by reading. A well-appointed library—one with a wide variety of levels, genres, titles, topics, languages, and media—enables students to find texts that suit their interests and needs.

In the classroom library, students should have plenty of texts to choose from all year long. The library should be arranged for easy access and navigation to promote engagement. Bins clustered by genre, author, and topic help students find books they need and want to read. If students have access to tablets, be sure you create time to organize for how students are integrating both on and offline reading into library routines. Engage students in organizing and contributing parts of the library. One easy way to do this is to allow them to form "Our Favorites" baskets with their favorite trade books or baskets of their own writing, all to encourage others to read.

Text Types to Consider for Your Classroom Library			
Narrative	**Informational**	**Opinion/Argument**	**Poetry**
• Fairy tales • Myths • Graphic novels • Science fiction • Fantasy stories • Poetry • Realistic fiction • Historical fiction • Short stories • Memoir • Blogs	• Primary source documents • Reports • Informative picture books • Blogs • Biographies • Journal articles • Infographics • Functional texts • Scientific texts • Mathematical texts • Magazine articles • Websites • Historical texts • Maps	• Editorials • Reviews: product, music, film, book • Blogs • Social media posts • Letters to the editor • Advertisements	• Odes • Sonnets • Free verse • Haiku • Cinquains • Couplets • Songs • Lullabies

The 7 Strengths and the Classroom Library

- Highlight belonging by including texts that capture the mirrors and windows of human experience.

- Deepen curiosity by offering children a diverse and interesting collection.

- Develop curiosity by including texts that are not commonly found in classroom libraries, but children love to read because they truly reflect their interests, such as sports books and silly joke books.

- Build children's capacity for kindness by offering them a wide variety of books containing characters and true-life heroes who go above and beyond for other people.

Mentor Texts

What Is It? Well-written texts that are used as models to influence students' reading and writing, or inspire students personally.

Why Are Mentor Texts Helpful to Super Readers? To mentor is to teach. Super readers often have favorite texts that influence or inspire them in important, sometimes profound ways. For example, they may relate to a character or theme so strongly that they will articulate that the book changed their lives or the way they think about themselves. Informational texts may be mentor texts as well, especially those to which a reader turns time and time again for knowledge that enhances some aspect of their life. Some readers find a text they love so much that it provokes a turning point in their lives as a reader. They may even credit it for teaching them to read or making them think of themselves as readers for the first time.

Mentor texts may also impact a reader's writing life. All writers are readers. By definition, great writers have to be readers of other's texts and close and careful readers of the texts they create. Unfortunately, not all readers see themselves as writers and we'd like to change that. Ernest's life was forever changed by a fourth-grade teacher who allowed him to write his own novel. As we allow our students to write in the artistic genres that they read, we will create the conditions for very close reading. When we've given the opportunity for fourth graders to write plays responding to social issues they'd like to change, they become very close readers of plays as a way to learn the genre. They also become close readers of the news and of research that deals with social issues that matter to them, such as environmental threats, global hunger, and bullying on school campuses.

Writers learn to write by noticing what authors do. Reading fantastic, exemplar texts teaches them how to…

- Begin a story
- Teach something new
- Gather facts that build an idea
- Understand someone's feelings
- Make language beautiful
- Prove a point
- Build imaginary worlds
- Make a reader laugh
- End a story

The 7 Strengths and Mentor Texts

- Form book clubs based on favorite authors or genres (e.g., fantasy, historical fiction, comic books) to foster a sense of belonging.

- Encourage students to be curious about authors—why they write, where they get their inspiration, why they make the literary choices they do, and so on.

- Help students to develop the courage to try out new genres, styles, or topics inspired by their mentor texts.

Best practices become even better when they are rooted in the 7 Strengths. When social-emotional learning is seamlessly folded into the reading routines, students learn more effectively. Teaching structures such as the read aloud, close reading, and reading celebrations will help you to build the 7 Strengths in your students.

Now let us turn to the super practice of all practices, the key ingredient to raising a lifelong super reader: the practice of independent reading itself. We gave this practice a chapter all of its own because we want to be sure you take time to study it, implement it, and value it highly. It is often considered optional or supplemental, but as any super reader will tell you, this practice needs to be central: it is what turned them into lifelong readers. Let's find out how to integrate it into our instruction in magical, yet highly practical ways.

CHAPTER 11

INDEPENDENT READING: THE SUPER PRACTICE

Independent reading is the time a reader spends actively engaged in reading a wide range of text, with active support and related instruction from the teacher. Recommended daily independent reading time—20 minutes a day in school, 20 minutes in the after-school program, and 20 minutes at home—add up to one hour of transformational opportunity. Not bad for 60 minutes!

In the 7 Strengths Model, independent reading is at the core of everything and is directly connected to instruction. Every minute children read allows them to develop a strong reading identity as well as stamina and fluency that leads to a lifelong love of reading.

The Importance of Choice and Access

Choice is crucial. It is important to give children the agency to discover their interests, likes, and dislikes as readers in order to build their identities as readers. When children choose their own texts, they feel a further sense of belonging and identity to a reading community.

Children must also have access to a wide variety of diverse texts to read that are easy, just right, and difficult to decode, all of which have some purpose for the growing reader. Easy books provide practice toward fluency. Just-right texts familiarize students with the sensation of comprehension, deeper analysis, and enjoyment of texts intended for them. Difficult books, which should be of high interest to the readers, push students to decode more complex texts.

Of course, we all read for many other purposes than to practice reading, so students need these opportunities as well. It may be they are seeking information. It may be that they need a book with a strong character to participate in a discussion about point of view. It may be they want to read a book their friend is reading. It may be they love an author and want to read everything the author has written. The classroom library should allow for all of these possibilities.

Providing students with opportunities for choice and access to the right texts requires a purposefully organized classroom library. Students need some guidance and scaffolding about how to make the right choices for themselves as readers, so help them become familiar with the various sections of your library, and ensure that all students know where to find the texts they seek.

Independent reading should be purposeful and directly linked to instruction. Each day, help students engage in their reading with clear expectations about the work they should do. What was the point made in the lesson? Was it a process lesson that taught the behaviors of real readers? Was it a strategy lesson that provided students with a specific reading strategy? Or was it a lesson rooted in content from academic standards? The independent reading should provide students with the opportunity to practice the skills that were addressed in their instruction.

Mr. Sanchez was in the middle of a unit of study on finding life lessons in novels. He demonstrated how readers notice when a character changes in some significant way in order to identify the life lesson that may be present in the book. He asked his class to find examples of characters who have changed in other books. He told his class that in today's independent reading, they should each read a story and notice when the main character changes and see if this reveals one of the life lessons in the story. Some students used sticky notes and others used their tech devices to jot notes about their thoughts as they read. Later, Mr. Sanchez brought the students back together to discuss their ideas about the life lessons they discovered in their stories.

Independent reading should be a time of active, accountable learning for both teacher and students, as everyone works together to build engagement, motivation, and dynamic academic achievement. Strong independent readers will curate their own ever-growing, ever-changing reading collections. They will show interest in learning new words and phrases, building their reading stamina as they become lost in the world of their text. Strong independent readers discuss their own reading and actively listen to the ideas of other readers. They generate high-level inquiry questions and answer inferential questions with textual evidence. Strong independent readers are super readers.

What do students do during independent reading?

- Choose from a selection of high-interest texts.
- Read!
- Practice skills they are learning as a whole class.
- May connect thinking/discussion to shared ideas from a whole-class reading.
- Participate in conversations with partners about central ideas or shared texts.

Recommended Minimum Minutes for Daily Independent Reading*	
Grade	**Minutes**
K	10
1	15
2	20
3	25
4	30
5	30
6–8	20–30 given the constraints of a middle school schedule

*These are approximations. Use your judgment based on what you know about your students.

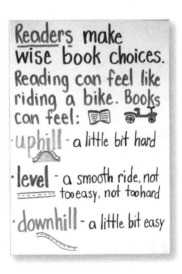

What do teachers do during independent reading time?

- Confer with individual students to further their skills.
- Coach discussions students are having in a partner talk.
- Help students choose books for their independent reading plans.
- Instruct small groups of students with similar challenges and strengths.
- Gather formative assessment data.

Taking a close look at the 7 Strengths helps us organize goals for independent reading:

Strength	In a 7 Strengths Classroom...
BELONGING	Children work together to create a reading community to explore a world of knowledge and a diverse body of literature.
CURIOSITY	Children feed their curious minds by having a chance to select their own reading materials and ask and answer questions to pursue their genuine wonderings.
FRIENDSHIP	Children bond through shared reading passions, building identity as readers, and working collaboratively.
KINDNESS	Children support one another across reading levels, working together to reach new dimensions as readers.
CONFIDENCE	Children practice reading at uphill levels (more challenging), downhill levels (less challenging), and just-right levels, making their own choices based on interest, passion, and purpose.
COURAGE	Children see challenge as part of the reading process and work through the hard parts with fortitude, perseverance, and determination.
HOPE	Children set goals for themselves as readers, and set goals for how reading can change their lives and the lives of others.

Why Should Independent Reading Connect Deeply to Explicit Instruction?

The connection between explicit instruction in reading and what students practice during independent reading time is the cornerstone of effective instruction. Students must be taught essential skills and strategies and be given time to apply what they have learned. That way, they develop the reading capacities that curricular standards demand of them. It is not sufficient for students to simply be sent off to "free read." Unstructured reading time and practices such as D.E.A.R. have benefits, but they don't provide the focused practice that most students need to stay engaged and learn what they need to learn.

Connect what you model during a lesson and what students practice during subsequent independent reading time. For example, you may use a sample informational text to model how readers use headings to determine what a part of the text will be about. Then, students would read informational texts independently for a large portion of the class period, paying attention to how the headings are helping them. They might have to highlight a couple of headings they found and be prepared to describe how they used the headings. These results may be shared in student notes for the teacher to see and/or during a whole-class discussion at the end of the period. The teacher may be reading aloud from *Charlotte's Web* as a whole-class instructional text, looking closely at the connection between characters and theme. The students may then be looking for similar connections in their own independent reading texts. This practice of accountable independent reading will yield much better results than unstructured reading time.

A Word About Stamina

Stamina is the most underrated yet crucial element of how super readers build their muscles. As with sports, the athlete builds capacity by building minutes. Every minute added to the practice, every breath taken, makes the athlete stronger. Call attention to stamina-building in your classroom of super readers. Honor it, value it, and affirm it. Here are two examples of how you can support it:

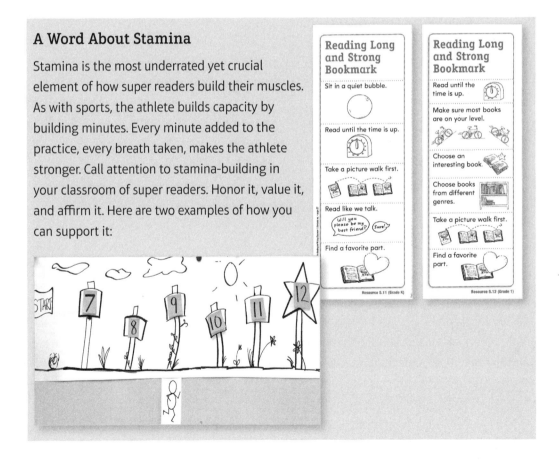

One-to-One Reading Conversations/Conferring

What Is It? A focused conversation between an adult and a child that explores the child's thinking and conclusions about a text and possible strategies to enhance understanding and engagement during independent reading time.

Why Are Reading Conversations Helpful to Super Readers? The standards, research of best practices, and demands of college and career all point to more of an inquiry-based approach to how children learn to talk about books. It is important therefore that we create time each day to talk one-to-one with our children about their reading lives during independent reading. These conversations should feature a great deal of active listening from adults. In fact, active listening will help us to be the best advocates and champions of super readers we can be. (See page 184 for a conferring checklist to use to assess students.)

We can invite children—even the youngest children—to use the 7 Strengths by asking them the questions below when we confer with them.

Strength	Questions to Ask While Conferring With Students
BELONGING	• How do you connect to the world of this story? • How did you reach out to someone as a reader today or this week?
CURIOSITY	• What are you wondering about? • What are you learning about?
FRIENDSHIP	• Was there a way you listened deeply to another reader today? • How can our classmates be better reading friends toward each other?
KINDNESS	• How did you help someone as a learner today? • Is there a character who has taught you a lesson about kindness?
CONFIDENCE	• How are you building reading skills? • What did you read today that made you feel like a bolder person overall?
COURAGE	• How did you share in discussion today in a way that felt brave? • What did you try in your reading that felt brave?
HOPE	• What are your goals for yourself as a reader?

Writing About Reading

What Is It? Students engage in writing in response to a text, which allows them to articulate and process their thinking or share their thinking with a wider audience.

Why Is Writing About Reading Helpful to Super Readers? Writing about reading can deepen the reading experience. It should not be done with every text a student reads or every time a student reads during independent reading, but used wisely and with exceedingly good judgment, it can truly enhance a child's experience with text. We have identified five major categories:

Analytical writing: Students can write book reviews, literary essays, character sketches, and author profiles. These can be written in response to any reading genre.

Creative writing: Students can craft original, creative literary responses, such as a poem, an alternate ending, an interview, or a play inspired by the reading.

Critical insights: Students can draw critical insights to question or interrogate texts where they may see a bias present that troubles some conclusions that the text has drawn.

Self-evaluative writing: Students can self-evaluate to identify reading preferences, set goals, and reflect on strategy use and general growth as a reader.

Extension writing: Students can also tap into their curiosity and use the text as a springboard to inquiry and further research about a topic or theme they have found compelling. Perhaps a story about a historical character has inspired them to do their own historical research on their family or community. Or maybe a story that deals with science or technology has inspired them to conduct their own scientific investigations.

Supporting Striving Readers

The following strategies are helpful to all students, but most particularly to striving readers:

- Focus on the positive.
- Have books that they can take home to practice reading.
- Provide "just-right" books they can read and take home to practice.
- Value high-level thinking with lower-level text.

- Think about genres, authors, text type, environment, and other factors to *spark motivation*.

- Build stamina with multiple texts (instead of just one) during independent reading time.

- Model the following reading strategies:

  - Look at the illustrations to figure out the word(s).

  - Sound out the word.

  - Chunk the word (look for shorter words within longer words).

  - Skip the word (return to it later).

  - Flip the vowel sound.

  - Finger point.

- Use technology to increase student engagement and ease of response.

Supporting Emerging Bilinguals

The following strategies are helpful to all students, but most particularly to emerging bilinguals:

- Partner wisely. Make sure children have a variety of partners to turn and talk to so they can practice developing English skills with many different kinds of speakers and listeners. Create flexible reading partnerships so emerging bilinguals can work with other emerging bilinguals and also with native English speakers.

- Read aloud every day. Model and marinate emerging bilinguals in new English grammar and vocabulary.

- Use visuals. As you read aloud, be sure children can clearly see the images on the pages. If possible, display images on the wall or screen, using a digital projector. Value the children's interpretation of the art and the photographs—it's all part of reading development.

- Celebrate mistakes. When learning a language, children often make very wise errors based on what they know about their native language. Praise and point this out when you see that happening. For example, a child who puts an adjective after a noun instead of before it who is a native Spanish speaker is making a very logical choice.

- Encourage rereading. Emerging bilinguals need abundant opportunities to revisit text. Rereading a text or revisiting a familiar text helps to reinforce language structures and new vocabulary for a child. Have partners reread read alouds to each other. Celebrate rereading of familiar texts.

- Honor students reading below grade level. Promote their oral language and critical thinking by challenging them to talk critically about lower-level texts.

- Make conversations matter. Help emerging bilinguals develop their oral communication skills by modeling conversational turns, such as: "I'd like to add to what you are saying." "I'd like to build off what _____ said." "I am wondering about what you said." Put those turns on a chart for students' reference.

- Treat writing as thinking. Emerging bilinguals are not all struggling writers! In fact, writing can help them feel more confident about speaking aloud. Provide them with sticky notes, index cards, and technology; have them "think off the texts"; and use their notes when they speak aloud.

- Create word banks. Focus on academic language and words that trigger longer complex oral thought, such as "however" and "in addition."

- Ensure library collections include books in students' home languages when possible.

This chapter highlighted the importance of independent reading as a central feature of instruction to build super readers. In the next chapter, we share techniques for management of a classroom of independent, diverse, eclectic readers.

CHAPTER 12

MANAGEMENT TECHNIQUES FOR THE SUPER READER CLASSROOM

In a classroom full of super readers, children have strong voices and make a lot of choices. This is wonderful and exciting but it can also be challenging for the adults in charge. For those moments when you want to scream "Help!" here are some tried-and-true management tips.

Techniques to Promote Active Engagement for All Students

Turn and Talk

During a lesson, teachers may prompt students to turn to a partner and engage in a quick conversation to answer a question or share thoughts about a text. Because everyone is talking to a partner, far more students will be engaged in thinking about their reading. When we ask children to turn and talk, they are able to practice a skill, strategy, or behavior while you listen in to assess understanding and offer your assistance. Give children a couple of minutes to talk with a partner. Make sure the "Turn and Talk" partnerships change often to give children a chance to talk with a variety of peers.

Turn and Talk Procedure

Face your partner
Shoulders to shoulders
Knees to knees
Make eye contact
Listen respectfully
Participate in the conversation

Stop and Jot

A stop and jot gives students a chance to quickly record their thinking in writing to develop and gauge their understanding of the topic. By asking a meaningful question and allowing students to jot their response, you allow students the opportunity to demonstrate their understanding, identify any confusions, and develop their critical thinking skills.

Techniques to Control Noise Level

Quiet Bubble

We can't expect young children to be completely silent as they read and write. However, we can create a buzz that feels comfortable for everyone—one that allows students to focus on their work. One way to do that is with Quiet Bubble. When students are working, tell them to imagine that they are each reading or writing in a giant bubble of peaceful quiet. Loud voices or touching each other will pop the bubble. They must work hard to control their voice so they don't pop their own bubbles or anyone else's.

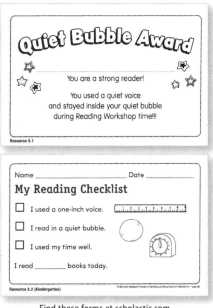

Find these forms at scholastic.com /superreaderresources.

One-Inch Voice

The term "one-inch voice" is also extremely helpful. Our students understand the visual of one inch and they can show you with their finger and thumb precisely how big that is. It helps them to have a visual because when adults say "Be quiet!" children often think they are being quiet! A reminder of the one-inch voice helps them to visualize just what you mean by *quiet*.

Silent Motions

To encourage active listening and a strong sense of community, teach your children to use hand signals. If a child has a question, she can raise two fingers together (index and middle) to let the speaker know that when she is finished, she has something to add. If children want to express that they feel the same way about what another person is describing, or have had the same experience, they can use the "me too" hand signal, making a fist, but holding out their pinkies and thumbs. The children then move their hands back and forth with their thumbs facing inward. Another hand signal you can use is "spirit fingers." When children appreciate others, they can hold their hands up by their shoulders with their palms facing out and fingers pointed up, and wiggle their fingers.

You can also use thumbs up/thumbs down as a quick assessment for understanding of instructions and/or concept. Non-verbal signals allow teachers to keep the flow of the lesson moving forward.

Techniques to Manage Partner and Group Work

A and B Partners

Before asking students to work in pairs, plan who will be in each partnership. Once you have done that, make one partner the A partner and one the B partner. (You may also use colors, numbers, shapes, and so on, to designate the different roles in the partnership.) Then you can easily refer to the partners to give directions. For example:

> *Sit on the rug with your partners. As should sit on the side closest to the window.*
> *Turn to your partner and answer the question. Bs answer first, then As.*
> *As bring a dictionary or tablet to the rug. Bs bring a small whiteboard and a marker.*
> *Today Bs will read aloud to As.*

Clock Buddies

Clock Buddies is a great tool for managing partner work in reading. Students get to set up their own partnerships using the simple clock visual, in which the hours of the clock identify a different partner. At the beginning of a school year, instruct students to select a partner for each blank slot on their clock. Circulate the classroom to help ensure that both partners copy their names in the appropriate lines. Once the pairings are established, you can assign tasks like partner reading, conferring, or share-outs. For example, "Today, you will be buddy reading with your 3 o'clock partner." This strategy helps promote engagement and collaboration between different students in a class.

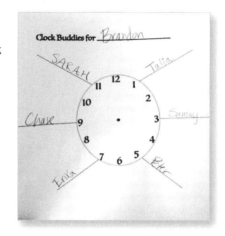

5 Ways to Recognize Good Work

1. **Call-Out** During independent reading or writing practice, request a quick call-out. During the call-out, when you have students' attention, highlight a specific student as an example of great work or great behavior. "I love how Sarah helped her partner find a book."

2. **7 Strengths Awards** Provide awards centered around the 7 Strengths. For example, the Curiosity Award could be given to a student who asks a question that leads to an interesting discussion.

3. **Shooting Stars** Send "shooting stars" to a student who took any kind of step, large or small, as a reader. Pantomime throwing a handful of sparkling stars at the student while encouraging him or her to "catch" them.

4. **Snap Claps** Have the class or a small group give a student a round of "snap claps" (rapid finger snapping) for a quick and quiet way to affirm good work. (It is less disruptive than regular claps!)

5. **Partner Awards** Affirm the work reading partners do together by giving weekly awards to effective partnerships.

Available at scholastic.com/superreaderresources.

Who Gets a Turn?

Place one labeled popsicle stick into a can for every student in the class. Select a stick from the can whenever you need to choose a student to share work, answer a question, or present to the class. Replace the sticks in the can for another "round" only after every stick has been selected.

Techniques to Facilitate Transitions

Student Call and Response

Engage students in rousing call and response chants at key points during the day. For example, the following can be used to transition into reading time on the rug or independent reading.

Student: *Ready to read? (Clap, clap)*

Class: *Read to read! (Clap, clap)*

Student: *Get what you need! (Clap, clap)*

Class: *Get what we need! (Clap, clap)*

Student: *Sit in your nook! (Clap, clap)*

Class: *Find your book! (Clap, clap)*

Student: *Ready to go! (Clap, clap)*

Class: *Ready to go! (Clap, clap)*

Musical Transitions

Use a specific song or musical instrument to signal to students when it is time to transition from one activity to another. For example, play a soothing song to let students know when independent reading is coming to a close or a peppy song when it is time for students to choose books from the classroom library. Students quickly learn to associate the song with the segment of the lesson or the activity and smoothly transition.

> **READERS' SONG**
> **(to the tune of "Twinkle, Twinkle, Little Star")**
>
> We know when we hear
> this rhyme
> It's our song for Reading Time.
> Reading love is in my heart
> Everyone will do their part.
> Check the chart for
> where to go
> Reading Time, I love you so!

Tech Transitions

Classroom management routines are important throughout the school day. This includes moments when technology is used during instruction. For example, when asking students to remove a tablet or laptop from a class cart, provide a pathway in your classroom for students to easily walk up and grab their devices before finding their seats. Practice this procedure the same way you would have students practice lining up for recess or moving from their desks to the rug. Reinforce literacy and numeracy concepts by asking students with a device labeled with an even number or whose first name starts with a certain letter to line up first. If you want to make sure students are listening to directions before a transition (instead of staring at their devices), ask them to close their laptops or flip over their tablets so eyes stay on the speaker. Build this into your everyday routines the same way students know when to take out a reading folder or grab a book from their book baggies.

Management Techniques for Small-Group Time

When to Interrupt

In their eagerness to share their findings, wonderings, ideas, and discoveries, students often interrupt teachers who are working with small groups. Clearly explain when it is okay to interrupt and when it isn't. Also, provide students with clear directions for what they can do when you are busy in a conference or small-group meeting. Create charts and hang them around the room, which might be titled "What to Do When You Think You Are Done," or "What to Do When You Need Help From the Teacher." List options such as the following:

- Reread the paragraph/section of their book.
- Ask a partner a question.
- Put their question on a sticky note for when they have their conference.
- Sign up for a conference.
- Choose a new book to read.

If students know what to do when a teacher is busy and feel confident that their questions or ideas will be addressed later on, they will learn to not interrupt.

Red Light, Green Light

When working with a small group, the teacher displays a cardboard traffic light. Red means "In conference." Green means "Free now."

Conferring Hat

When conferring with students, the teacher wears a special hat or bracelet that means "Please know I am in a conference and would prefer to stay focused here unless you really need me right away."

Two Then Me

Before approaching the teacher for help on a reading task, students are encouraged to ask two other friends for assistance first.

Tech Tips for Managing Others

1. Introduce new tech tools to a small group of students and let them become the "experts" before a whole-class lesson.
2. Create instructions with screenshots to leave at stations where students will work in partners or independently.
3. Label student devices with names and numbers using colorful tape or stickers.

Techniques for Keeping Students Focused and Engaged

Every classroom has students who have a more difficult time staying on task and engaging fully 100 percent of the time in the planned activities. Off-task behavior can be kept to a minimum with a little effort and strategy on your part. Consider the following three techniques:

Make learning tools accessible and readily available.

A 7 Strengths classroom belongs to the student. Make sure the classroom library or online texts students need to carry out expected tasks are accessible and well organized. If you want students to write about their reading easily and fluidly, give them baskets of sticky notes, personalized notebooks, and tablets and other digital devices to reach for on their own.

Make routines familiar and stick with them.

We've made the case for reading routines, but be sure to stick with them! Use similar transitions to and from reading time every day. Plan around the whole-small-whole model every day as well. The more "sameness" in the routine, the better. Students will settle into these predictable structures of their day and will show less off-task behavior when the expectations are clear.

Communicate clear expectations for daily reading work.

Posting anchor charts and providing tech support can help students remember and keep focused on the expectations. You can create a folder with pictures of anchor charts students can access on their laptops or a QR code they scan with a tablet that connects to an online resource for extra help.

Walking into a classroom of super readers can be deceiving. A sense of calm, students on task, a busy hum—these classrooms almost seem to run on their own. The trained eye, however, can see the amount of teaching and foundational work that went into creating an environment such as this, where every member of the community is engaged and learning. These management strategies will help you create such an environment, a true and trusting community in which every child is a super reader.

Next, we will share with you formative assessment tools that will help you see your students through many important lenses and teach in ways that are deeply supportive of their growth.

CHAPTER 13

ASSESSMENT TOOLS FOR THE SUPER READER CLASSROOM

In this chapter, we share with you some innovative ways to assess your students formatively on their journeys to becoming super readers.

SEE PAGE 174.

7 Strengths Student Survey

7 Strengths Student Survey allows you to learn detailed information about the child's opinion of him- or herself as a reader.

Super Reader Rubric

The Super Reader Rubric enables you to keep a running observational record of many super reading skills. Use it as you watch your readers in action and as you prepare a collective data picture of your students. This rubric is based on an asset model, so it will help guide you to notice those skills your students can already do so that you can plan next goals and next steps for them.

SEE PAGES 176–179.

7 Strengths Checklist for Digital Citizenship

Engaging online is exciting and complex. We can use the 7 Strengths to foster digital citizenship in a way all children can understand. The checklist we have created ensures that they are giving and receiving information online thoughtfully and caringly.

SEE PAGE 175.

Strength-Specific Goal-Setting Sheets

After you've gathered data on your super readers using the Student Survey, Super Reader Rubric, and Checklist for Digital Citizenship, use it to inform your instructional planning and differentiate instruction for every super reader. Analyze your data, looking for patterns of learning behavior and areas of need. Then work together to identify goals for each student for each strength, using the Strength-Specific Goal-Setting Sheets.

SEE PAGES 180–183.

Goal-Tracking Checklist

The Goal-Tracking Checklist can help you record goals for your super readers and the progress they have made toward mastery.

SEE PAGE 183.

Conferring Checklist for Independent Reading

Conferring is the best possible formative assessment there is. You can delve into the nuances of each child's reading progress. You can help the child set reading goals. The Conferring Checklist for Independent Reading helps you do that. See page 159 for more information on conferring with students.

SEE PAGE 184.

Super Reader Log

A reading log can be a useful assessment and accountability tool as you manage your super readers' independence. Students can fill out the Super Reader Log regularly as they engage in the reading routines and work in the classroom, after school, and at home. The Super Reading Log is a twist on the traditional reading log because it infuses the 7 Strengths into the reading work.

SEE PAGE 185.

These assessment tools are intended to be used to inform your teaching. (Find digital versions at scholastic.com/superreaderresources.) Watch and observe your students and record your impressions. Seek the opinions of your students as well. Then analyze the information you gather to set specific goals for each child. Track your students' progress toward their goals as well as to ensure that all readers develop an understanding of the 7 Strengths and grow into the super readers you know they can become.

7 Strengths Student Survey

BELONGING

Describe a reading community to which you belong.

Who do you talk to about your reading?

Where do you feel you fit in as a reader?

CURIOSITY

How does reading help you when you feel curious about something?

How does reading make you curious?

What reading tools do you use when you want to find out about something?

FRIENDSHIP

Describe one of your reading friends.

Describe someone whose recommendations you admire as a reader.

KINDNESS

What is one way you have learned about kindness through reading?

What is one way you have shown kindness to a fellow reader?

CONFIDENCE

How have you grown stronger as a reader?

What makes you proud of your reading?

Describe when you felt confident during reading time.

COURAGE

What is one way you have taken a chance as a reader?

How does reading help you feel brave?

HOPE

What are your hopes and dreams for yourself as a reader?

In what ways does reading help you feel hopeful?

7 Strengths Checklist for Digital Citizenship

Strength	Task	I did it!	I'm working on it.
BELONGING	I contributed a post to an online community.	☐	☐
KINDNESS	I added a positive comment to someone's post.	☐	☐
COURAGE	I took a risk by sharing an opinion online.	☐	☐
CURIOSITY	I searched for answers online.	☐	☐
FRIENDSHIP	I offered a suggestion or constructive criticism in an online community.	☐	☐
CONFIDENCE	I tried something new that I learned online.	☐	☐
HOPE	I set goals for participating in an online community.	☐	☐

Super Reader Rubric

	EMERGING	APPROACHING	ACHIEVING	EXCEEDING
	An emerging student is in the earliest stages of meeting the demands of the indicator. The student requires a large amount of scaffolding to be successful.	An approaching student demonstrates some success with the demands of the indicator. The student requires some scaffolding to be successful.	An achieving student demonstrates solid success with the demands of the indicator. The student exhibits independence and little or no scaffolding.	An exceeding student demonstrates exemplary success with the demands of the indicator. The student exhibits a high level of independence.
ENGAGEMENT AND ENJOYMENT	• Demonstrates emerging interest in reading. • Begins to connect read alouds to his or her own ideas. • Begins to name favorite books. • Begins to read through pictures (and possibly some text) with interest. • Begins to choose books based on familiarity with or interest in topic. • Begins to offer opinions about books. • Begins to read by choice during free or choice time.	• Sometimes demonstrates interest in reading. • Connects read alouds to his or her own ideas and conversations. • Names favorite books and/or passages or pictures from books. • Sometimes reads text or reads pictures with focus. • Sometimes chooses books based on familiarity with or interest in topic. • Offers occasional opinions about texts.	• Consistently demonstrates interest in reading. • Makes connections between read alouds, independent reading, and conversations. • Names favorite books, authors, and genres. • Builds minutes of independent reading time. • Chooses books based on passions, interests, and favorite authors. • Offers opinions about texts.	• Demonstrates strong interest in reading. • Makes insightful connections between read alouds, independent reading, and conversations; discusses the text's ideas, themes, and structures. • Shows excitement about favorite books, authors, and genres; revisits favorite texts. • Reads voraciously, is not easily distracted, and can quickly become "lost in the reading world." • Makes strong, well-informed reading choices based on passions and interests, favorite genres, and favorite authors. • Offers strong, well-informed opinions about texts and recommends books to others.

	EMERGING	APPROACHING	ACHIEVING	EXCEEDING
FLUENCY AND EXPRESSION	• Demonstrates emerging ability to read text fluently. • Begins to read words in isolation. • Begins to read with some expression. • Begins to heed punctuation.	• Sometimes reads text fluently. • Sometimes reads with appropriate phrasing. • Sometimes reads with appropriate expression. • Sometimes heeds punctuation.	• Consistently reads text fluently. • Often reads with appropriate phrasing. • Often reads with appropriate expression. • Often heeds punctuation.	• Demonstrates strong ability to read text fluently. • Always reads with exemplary phrasing. • Always reads with expression that indicates deep understanding of text. • Always uses punctuation to improve fluency and expression.
FOCUS AND STAMINA	• Demonstrates emerging ability to focus on reading. • Begins to stick with a text for a sustained time period. • Begins to self-regulate while reading to stay focused. • Reads for a small number of the recommended minutes* for the grade level.	• Sometimes demonstrates ability to focus on reading. • Sometimes sticks with a text for a sustained period of time. • Sometimes self-regulates while reading to stay focused. • Reads for some of the recommended minutes* for the grade level.	• Consistently demonstrates ability to focus on reading. • Consistently sticks with a text for a sustained period of time. • Consistently self-regulates while reading to stay focused, tuning out distractions. • Reads for most of the recommended minutes* for the grade level.	• Demonstrates exemplary ability to remain focused on reading. • Always sticks with a text, often requesting more reading time. • Always self-regulates while reading to stay focused, tuning out distractions, and losing him- or herself in the text. • Reads for more than the recommended minutes* for the grade level.
COMPREHENSION AND CRITICAL THINKING	• Demonstrates emerging comprehension and analysis of text. • Begins to identify ideas in texts. • Begins to ask clarifying questions to comprehend texts. • Begins to make connections between texts and the real world.	• Sometimes comprehends and analyzes texts. • Sometimes expresses ideas about texts. • Sometimes asks clarifying questions to comprehend texts. • Sometimes makes connections between texts and the world.	• Consistently comprehends and analyzes texts. • Consistently expresses ideas about texts. • Consistently asks clarifying questions to comprehend texts. • Consistently makes connections between texts and the real world.	• Demonstrates strong ability to comprehend and analyze texts. • Articulates ideas about texts clearly and completely. • Regularly analyzes texts and asks clarifying questions to improve comprehension. • Regularly makes deep connections between texts and the real world.

	EMERGING	APPROACHING	ACHIEVING	EXCEEDING
COLLABORATION AND COMMUNITY BUILDING	• Demonstrates emerging speaking and listening skills in partner or whole-group discussions. • Begins to participate in turn and talks. • Begins to engage in partner contributions. • Begins to participate in group discussions. • Begins to apply basic listening skills to engage partners. • Begins to balance listening and speaking in partner discussions. • Begins to express ideas inspired by read alouds.	• Sometimes speaks and listens in partner and whole-group discussions. • Shares during turn and talks. • Responds to partners' contributions. • Participates in group discussions. • Demonstrates active listening skills by expressing interest in the subject and responding to who's speaking. • Calibrates the balance of listening and speaking with a partner. • Shares ideas from read alouds that help unify the community.	• Consistently speaks and listens in partner and whole-group discussions. • Consistently shares during turn and talks. • Responds to and builds on peers' contributions. • Participates in group discussions and enriches the conversation with his or her contributions. • Demonstrates active listening skills such as showing interest in the topic and engaging in the discussion; reiterating what a partner expresses; perhaps using sentence starters such as, "I want to add on to what you are saying…" "I appreciate what you are saying…" and "I'm wondering about…" • Calibrates the balance of listening and speaking with a partner and in whole group. • Shares ideas from read alouds that help the community develop the 7 Strengths.	• Demonstrates exemplary speaking and listening skills in partner and whole-group discussions. • Shares during turn and talks; offers comments that enhance and deepen the conversation. • Responds to and builds on peers' contributions. • Participates in group discussions and enriches the conversation with his or her contributions; draws in peers by asking them questions. • Demonstrates active listening skills by leaning in and showing interest; continues discussions with comments such as, "I want to build off your idea…" and "I want to go back to what you said." • Calibrates the balance of speaking and listening with a partner and in whole group; actively listens and deepens speakers' ideas. • Shares ideas from read alouds and related discussions to foster growth of the community's 7 Strengths.

IDENTITY AND GOAL SETTING	EMERGING	APPROACHING	ACHIEVING	EXCEEDING
	• Shows emerging interest in identifying him- or herself as a reader, writer, speaker, listener, and learner.	• Sometimes names qualities of him- or herself as a reader, writer, speaker, listener and learner.	• Consistently names qualities of him- or herself as a reader, writer, speaker, and listener and learner; often connects to others as a fellow reader, writer, learner.	• Names many qualities of him- or herself as a reader, writer, learner.
	• Begins to connect to others as reader, writer, and learner.	• Sometimes connects to others as a fellow reader, writer, and learner.	• Identifies him- or herself as a reader; can name some reading preferences, strengths, and challenges.	• Strongly connects to others as a fellow reader, writer, speaker, listener, and learner.
	• Begins to identify him- or herself as a reader.	• Identifies self as a reader in contexts such as school.	• Can set some goals for him- or herself as a literacy learner and identify ways to meet those goals.	• Identifies him- or herself as a reader; can speak with ease about reading preferences, strengths, and challenges.
	• Begins to set a basic goal for him- or herself as a reader, writer, and learner.	• Sets one goal for him- or herself as a literacy learner.	• Views his or her own literacy skills through the lens of the 7 Strengths; applies lessons learned through reading and discussion to his or her own growth.	• Can set many goals for him- or herself as a literacy learner and lay out a plan to meet them; reflects on progress regularly.
	• Begins to view his or her own literacy skills through the lens of 7 Strengths.	• Views his or her own literacy skills through the lens of 7 Strengths; applies lessons learned through reading to frame ideas about him- or herself.	• Perseveres through challenging parts of reading, writing, speaking, and listening with self awareness; views challenges as opportunities for literacy growth.	• Views his or her own literacy skills through the lens of the 7 Strengths; regularly applies lessons learned through reading and discussion to his or her own growth; regularly seeks opportunities to grow stronger.
	• Begins to persevere when literacy work is challenging.	• Perseveres when literacy work is challenging.	• Identifies themes and lessons in literature and ideas from discussion; may think about and hope for change and progress in the world.	• Perseveres through challenging parts of reading, writing, speaking, and listening with self awareness; views challenges as opportunities for literacy growth; continuously gains new skills.
	• Begins to identify lessons in literature.	• Identifies themes and lessons in literature.		• Uses themes and lessons in literature and ideas from discussion to think about and hope for change and progress in the world.

*Recommended independent reading minutes per grade level: K: 10 minutes or more; Grade 1: 15 minutes or more; Grade 2: 20 minutes or more; Grade 3: 25 minutes or more; Grade 4: 30 minutes or more; Grade 5: 30 minutes or more; Grades 6–8: between 20–30 depending on class time

Goal Setting: Belonging

Task	I did it!	I'm working on it.	Notes
I have found a book buddy.	☐	☐	
I shared a favorite book with a classmate.	☐	☐	
I know what kind of books I like.	☐	☐	
I participate in a reading community by sharing my thoughts and listening to those of others.	☐	☐	
I praise and support other members of my reading community.	☐	☐	
I speak and listen in ways that make the community feel strong.	☐	☐	

Goal Setting: Kindness

Task	I did it!	I'm working on it.	Notes
I treat books with respect.	☐	☐	
I respect the opinions of others.	☐	☐	
I keep the classroom library clean.	☐	☐	
I listen with care.	☐	☐	
I take time to help someone else as a reader.	☐	☐	
I respect each person's book choices.	☐	☐	
I empathize with characters in stories.	☐	☐	

Goal Setting: Courage

Task	I did it!	I'm working on it.	Notes
I try different genres of books.	☐	☐	
I share my opinion with the class.	☐	☐	
I ask for help when I'm confused about what I read.	☐	☐	
I speak out with my ideas about reading.	☐	☐	
I listen deeply to ideas that may not always agree with mine.	☐	☐	
I take a chance to disagree with someone when I feel strongly about an idea.	☐	☐	
I push through the hard parts in my reading.	☐	☐	
I stand up for someone who is trying to express an opinion.	☐	☐	

Goal Setting: Curiosity

Task	I did it!	I'm working on it.	Notes
I ask questions about what I have read.	☐	☐	
I listen carefully when my peers share.	☐	☐	
I think about the author's purpose for writing a text.	☐	☐	
I look for answers to my questions in the text.	☐	☐	
I wonder about what an author has written.	☐	☐	
I question bias.	☐	☐	
I inquire about what I'm reading.	☐	☐	
I further my thinking by pursuing my questions across multiple texts.	☐	☐	

Goal Setting: Friendship

Task	I did it!	I'm working on it.	Notes
I give book recommendations.	☐	☐	
I listen respectfully to my peers' opinions.	☐	☐	
I ask for help when I'm confused.	☐	☐	
I reach out to help someone who needs reading support.	☐	☐	
I find themes in books that relate to big ideas about friendship.	☐	☐	
I invite someone to be my reading partner.	☐	☐	
I invite conversation around text that builds a feeling of connectedness.	☐	☐	

Goal Setting: Confidence

Task	I did it!	I'm working on it.	Notes
I talk about my opinions on favorite books.	☐	☐	
I present my writing to the class.	☐	☐	
I share how I feel about different characters.	☐	☐	
I read aloud to others.	☐	☐	
I share an idea I found in a text and build upon it.	☐	☐	
I invite others to share ideas.	☐	☐	
I learn about facts and use them to have a point of view in my conversations.	☐	☐	

Goal Setting: Hope

Task	I did it!	I'm working on it.	Notes
I set goals for myself as a reader.	☐	☐	
I identify characters with dreams.	☐	☐	
I know what type of reader I want to be.	☐	☐	
I create plans for myself as a reader, as a thinker, and as a dreamer.	☐	☐	
I believe I am someone who can change the world.	☐	☐	
I believe I can use what I learn and read to become better at positively influencing others.	☐	☐	

Goal-Tracking Checklist

Student Name:	Demonstrated Mastery	Working Toward Mastery	Requires Further Help	Next Steps (small-group work, conference, etc.)
Goal 1	☐	☐	☐	☐
Goal 2	☐	☐	☐	☐
Goal 3	☐	☐	☐	☐

Conferring Checklist for Independent Reading

Student Name: _____   Date: _____

Focus (circle one)	Observations	Next Steps
Engagement/ Enjoyment		
Stamina/Focus		
Fluency/Expression		
Comprehension/ Critical Thinking		
Collaboration/ Community Building		
Sense of Self/Identity as a Reader		

Super Reader Log

Name: _____   Date: _____

The 7 Strengths: Belonging, Curiosity, Friendship, Kindness, Confidence, Courage, and Hope

Title/Author	Type of Text	Stamina Meter	Engagement Meter	Enjoyment Meter
		1 hard to keep going **2** working on building minutes **3** read for full time	**1** not feeling very engaged **2** feeling a little engaged **3** feeling somewhat engaged **4** feeling highly engaged	**1** didn't enjoy **2** enjoyed a little bit **3** somewhat enjoyed **4** thoroughly enjoyed

When I read this text, I build the strength of _____ by

_____

When I read this text, I build the strength of _____ by

_____

When I read this text, I build the strength of _____ by

_____

CHAPTER 14

PLANNING TOOLS FOR THE SUPER READER CLASSROOM

Building a community of super readers happens all day, every day, as we provide space and support during school and out-of-school time. The 7 Strengths can help us plan a solid and structured year for super readers. Think big picture first by making an overall plan for how the year should be laid out, and then think more specifically day by day, hour by hour. What follows are planning tools to help you in this work. (For digital versions of checklists and record-keeping forms, go to scholastic.com/superreaderresources.)

Big-Picture Thinking

The following table provides big-picture thinking for promoting the 7 Strengths.

Strength	Big-Picture Thinking
BELONGING	Participate in community-building activities.
CURIOSITY	Be open to wonderings about self, the community, and the world.
FRIENDSHIP	Work in partnerships and small groups.
KINDNESS	Engage in social action reading/writing.
CONFIDENCE	Try new types of reading, learn to speak about one's reading.
COURAGE	Overcome struggle.
HOPE	Set goals for the week, month, year, and summer.

The First 25 Days

Here, we provide specific suggestions for the first 25 days of the school year for building a super reader classroom, using the 7 Strengths.

Day	Super Reader Task	We did it!	Notes/Next Steps
1	Build a community of readers by talking about favorite books.		
2	Build a community of readers by establishing speaking and listening routines.		
3	Build a community of readers by providing time to share favorite books.		
4	Help students choose books that are a good match.		
5	Help students open up to wonderings in a fictional text by making predictions and posing questions.		
6	Help students make personal connections to characters.		
7	Help students wonder about characters' (or real live people's) actions.		
8	Help students wonder about the theme or message of a book.		
9	Model how reading partners prepare for discussions.		
10	Model how reading partners listen to the contributions of their peers.		
11	Model how reading partners offer feedback.		
12	Help students open up to wonderings in the community interviewing real people.		
13	Help students open up to wonderings in the world by researching questions about current events.		
14	Help students take social action by exploring texts on world issues.		
15	Help students take social action by writing for an authentic audience.		
16	Model how to be brave by sticking with challenging books.		
17	Model how to be brave by asking for help.		
18	Model how to have confidence to use a variety of reading strategies to work through problems.		
19	Model how to try new genres including fiction, poetry, and informational text.		

20	Model how to try new authors.		
21	Model how to try new reading partners.		
22	Show students how to set a goal for weekly progress.		
23	Show students how to set a reading goal for the school year.		
24	Show students how to set a reading goal for any out-of-school time.		
25	Celebrate accomplishments—big and small!		

Sample Schedules

You may have a wonderful flow of the day already in place. But if you don't, here are some sample schedules for in-school and out-of-school time.

Sample Elementary School Schedule

8:30-8:40	**Arrival**	Have students unpack and settle in.
8:40-8:50	**Morning Meeting**	Engage the class in community-building activity.
8:50-9:10	**Interactive Read Aloud**	Introduce new book and lead students in a discussion.
9:10-9:20	**Partner Reading**	Have students read in partners or complete an activity based on the read aloud.
9:20-10:00	**Reading Workshop**	Follow a whole-small-whole model: whole-group mini-lesson, small-group and independent practice, whole-group share.
10:00-10:40	**Writing Workshop**	Follow a whole-small-whole model: whole-class mini-lesson, small-group and independent practice, whole-class share.
10:40-11:00	**Word Work**	Facilitate skill-set instruction: phonics, vocabulary.
11:00-12:00	**Lunch and Recess**	Free play and organized activities.
12:00-12:45	**Math Lesson**	Encourage students to write, speak, and listen.
12:45-1:15	**Centers/Choice Time**	Connect centers to the 7 Strengths; provide opportunities for group and partner work.
1:15-2:00	**Special/Cluster**	Provide specialized instruction in art, music, dance, gym.
2:00-2:45	**Content Area**	Facilitate Science and Social Studies activities that include: reading, writing, speaking, listening, and viewing.
2:45-3:00	**Good-bye Meeting**	Use activity connected to one of the 7 Strengths (may rotate weekly, monthly).

Sample Middle School Schedules

In middle school, the number of minutes allotted for English Language Arts (ELA) varies significantly. 100 to 120 minutes per day is optimal for thorough instruction and practice in reading and writing. Regardless of the amount of time you have, try this formula to ensure regular independent practice in reading and writing: Devote half the period to independent practice and devote the other half to a whole-class lesson and a whole-class wrap-up. Alternate between reading and writing across the week to balance the time. The sample schedules below follow this formula.

One 50-minute period per day for ELA

Day*	Monday (Reading)	Tuesday (Writing)	Wednesday (Reading)	Thursday (Writing)	Friday (Reading)
Whole-Class Lesson	20 minutes	20 minutes	20 minutes	20 minutes	20 minutes
Independent Practice	25 minutes	25 minutes	25 minutes	25 minutes	25 minutes
Wrap-Up	5 minutes	5 minutes	5 minutes	5 minutes	5 minutes

*The next week may switch to allow for three writing and two reading periods.

Two 50-minute periods per day for ELA

		Monday	Tuesday	Wednesday	Thursday	Friday
50-minute period #1	**Whole-Class Reading Lesson**	20 minutes	20 minutes	20 minutes	20 minutes	20 minutes
	Independent Reading Practice	25 minutes	25 minutes	25 minutes	25 minutes	25 minutes
	Reading Wrap-Up	5 minutes	5 minutes	5 minutes	5 minutes	5 minutes
50-minute period # 2	**Whole-Class Writing Lesson**	20 minutes	20 minutes	20 minutes	20 minutes	20 minutes
	Independent Writing Practice	25 minutes	25 minutes	25 minutes	25 minutes	25 minutes
	Writing Wrap-Up	5 minutes	5 minutes	5 minutes	5 minutes	5 minutes

Out-of-School Program

Below is a tried-and-true schedule for an after-school program designed to nurture super readers. There is plenty of time for reading together and independently, and sharing ideas with others.

3:00-3:05	**Transition Time**	Have students grab a snack and settle in.
3:05-3:10	**Welcome and Introduction**	Welcome students and establish goals for the day.
3:10-3:25	**Interactive Read Aloud**	Introduce new book and lead students in a discussion.
3:25-3:50	**Respond to Reading**	Conduct group activity connected to read aloud requiring writing/illustrating and text connections.
3:50-4:00	**Share Out and Transition**	Share student creations and transition to independent reading time.
4:00-4:30	**Independent Reading**	Facilitate independent reading and partner reading.
4:30-4:40	**Share Out**	Have students talk about their books with reading partners.
4:40-4:45	**Wrap-Up and Pack Up**	Have students gather belongings and clean up their reading spaces.

7 Strengths Partnership Checklist

This checklist guides students to bring the 7 Strengths to their work with partners.

Task	I did it!	I'm working on it.	Notes/Comments
BELONGING: I greet my partner and give a compliment.	☐	☐	
CURIOSITY: I ask questions about things my partner has to say.	☐	☐	
FRIENDSHIP: I show a connection when talking to my partner.	☐	☐	
KINDNESS: I listen to what my partner has to say.	☐	☐	
CONFIDENCE: I provide constructive feedback.	☐	☐	
COURAGE: I work with different people in my class—even if they're not my best friends.	☐	☐	
HOPE: I set reading goals with my partner.	☐	☐	

Short-Term Goal Template: Use this template to help students set and meet short-term reading goals. Encourage them to be specific and articulate how their goals will help them as readers.

Name: Date:		I did it!
What will you do to become a stronger reader this week?		☐
What will you do to become a stronger reader this month?		☐
Who can help you become a better reader? How?		☐

Long-Term Goal Guide: Use this guide to help students set long-term reading goals and visualize specific ways to achieve them. Once goals are set, check progress and revise or set new goals as necessary.

Name: Date:				
Reading Goal	**Target Date**	**How will I accomplish this goal?**	**Who can help me? How?**	**I did it!**
				☐
				☐
				☐
				☐
				☐

LitCamp Schedule

Scholastic and LitWorld have partnered to create an out-of-school solution to close the literacy gap. Here is the schedule for LitCamp, a summer curriculum for schools and community-based organizations. For information about LitCamp, visit www.scholastic.com/litcamp.

Opening Campfire (15 mins)	• Greeting • Community-Building Activity • Transition Song • Words of the Day • Materials
Read Aloud (25 mins)	• Interactive read aloud with fiction or nonfiction text
Bring the Text to Life (20 mins)	• Activity with listening and speaking objectives
Reading Power (25 mins)	• Skills-based activities related to the read-aloud text
Bunk Time: Independent Reading (20 mins)	• Books chosen by campers
Community Lit (15 mins)	• Game or conversational activity
Writing Power (15 mins)	• Writing activity aligned with the read-aloud text
Closing Campfire (15 mins)	• Word game • Reflections • Praise and affirmations

Our Yearlong Plan for Reading: Supporting All Children

Month	Focus for Super Readers	School-wide Goals for Super Readers	Action Plan	What Families Can Do
AUGUST	Super readers need a dedicated place to read that is welcoming and supportive.	Each classroom should have a dedicated reading area.	• Create a space for readers using a rug, beanbag chairs, or floor pillows. • Collect donations or hold a fund-raiser to purchase library resources.	Dedicate a special place at home for reading. This could include special floor pillows or a corner of a bedroom with posters of favorite books.
SEPTEMBER	Super readers have access to high-interest books in a variety of genres and levels.	Each classroom should have a library that contains books students are excited to read.	• Survey students. (See a sample survey on page 174) • Create a book wish list for your school. • Order books and solicit donations to grow your classroom library.	Make sure children have access to books at home. This could be accomplished through a rotating collection from the local library.
OCTOBER	Super readers use anchor charts and reference tools to help grow their independence.	Students use reference materials to help them strengthen their ability to read independently.	• Identify what reading behaviors foster independence in your students. • Create resources (e.g., bookmarks, anchor charts) that students can refer to when reading. • Make sure that reference materials are accessible for all students.	Support children at home by making connections to skills and reading behaviors taught in the classroom.
NOVEMBER	Super readers read print and digital text.	Students are introduced to digital texts to help them become lifelong readers in a high-tech world.	• Determine what types of technology students have access to at home and in school. • Locate digital texts from online publications and libraries that are appropriate for students. • Provide text choice for readers that includes tablets and computers.	Introduce children to digital texts on smartphones, tablets, and computer screens. Families can model this behavior by making connections to their own reading.

DECEMBER	Super readers have goals for lifelong reading.	Students should be able to articulate reading goals they've set with teacher and family input.	• Have conversations about goal setting. • Develop goals with students on how they will work to grow as readers. • Create an action plan for student goals that include time to check in on their progress.	Urge families to model lifelong reading behaviors such as reading together as a family and talking about books.
JANUARY	Super readers have reading buddies to talk to about their favorite books.	Students talk about their favorite books with peers.	• Develop protocols for sharing favorite books with student input. • Establish reading groups and partnerships. • Provide time for students to talk about books.	Offer book clubs for families or nights where families can come and share favorite books.
FEBRUARY	Super readers share their opinions about books.	Students have opinions about books, which they share in many ways.	• Teach students how to form and support an opinion. • Give students options for how to share their opinions. • Provide an authentic audience for students.	Ask families to post their favorite books on an online school page or add their favorites to a school bulletin board.
MARCH	Super readers put what they've learned into action.	You make a change in the community based on ideas you've learned from your own reading.	• Decide on a community issue you'd like to address with students. • Read together to learn more about it. • Develop an action plan to make a change in your community.	Bring families together for a community action project based on student reading explorations.
APRIL	Super readers keep track of their reading and know what books they want to read next.	Students keep track of their reading in a log and have a plan for their next books.	• Create a system that readers can use to keep track of their books. • Hold students accountable for keeping a log of their reading.	Have families monitor children's reading goals by checking in on progress in school and encouraging reading at home.

MAY	Super readers can name their favorite authors.	Students have been immersed in an author study and can name favorite writers.	• Determine authors the children love. • Encourage students to talk and write about their favorite authors.	Encourage families to have conversations about books and urge children to name their favorite authors.
JUNE	Super readers want to become lifelong readers.	Students view reading as an important part of their lives.	• Cultivate a joy of reading by creating time to talk about books and encouraging teachers to share books they love. • Invite guests to your classroom to talk about their own reading journeys.	Encourage families to identify their own reading goals to demonstrate how reading is a lifelong journey.
JULY	Super readers spend time with books outside of the classroom.	Students read with family members 365 days a year.	• Work with families to create reading plans for outside-of-school hours. • Support families through workshops and resources. • Provide access to quality texts so families can read together consistently.	Ask families to commit to reading goals over the summer.

7 STRENGTHS FOR EDUCATORS, 7 STRENGTHS FOR FAMILIES

A 7 Strengths-inspired wish for you, educators, to send you on your way:

BELONGING: That you will have the privilege of belonging to the world of educators who believe in all children as super readers and to the community of children who are becoming those readers.

CURIOSITY: That you will be inspired by children's curiosity and that you will be fueled by their extraordinary questions that will lead us to a better world.

FRIENDSHIP: That you deepen relationships both with the children you serve and the adults with whom you work, coming closer in understanding to each other through reading.

KINDNESS: That you will experience the power of kindness through the characters you meet in literature and through the actions you and your super readers take to make the world more beautiful.

CONFIDENCE: That you will have the confidence to learn and grow in your work and that you will inspire that same confidence in the growing super readers in your lives.

COURAGE: That you will have courage, on a day that feels hard, to try again and again, and that you will be fearless and resolved to work through the challenging aspects of creating a world of super readers.

HOPE: That you dream big dreams, that your literacy legacy will be eternal, that you cultivate dreamers and doers among your super readers that make the world a better place, and that through the work you do, we are all changed.

And a 7 Strengths-inspired wish for families as well:

BELONGING: That you will feel a sense of belonging to the wider community of families, loving your children into becoming super readers.

CURIOSITY: That you will feel the power of curiosity in asking your children questions about their reading lives.

FRIENDSHIP: That you learn with your child the power of friendship through stories and that through those models you can help your child forge lasting relationships with others.

KINDNESS: That you will touch and be touched by others in the kindness of everyday moments, that you will find them in the pages of books, and that together you and your child can touch others.

CONFIDENCE: That you will feel the power of confidence in your child as a reader, letting his or her wisdom and passions guide you the most.

COURAGE: That you will be courageous on a day that feels hard, try again and again, and work through the hard parts of raising a super reader.

HOPE: That you create hopes and dreams for and with your child as a reader, and that they all come true.

Appendix

Strength-Specific Children's Texts

To create super readers, you need to have a strong belief in the child and a multitude of high-quality books and poems available for them. We recognize how difficult it can be to develop a list of great literary selections that appeal to a range of readers. This appendix, organized according to the 7 Strengths, was inspired by our collective experiences as well as suggestions from colleagues whose opinions we dearly respect. Use these books and poems in your teaching, give them to children for their reading pleasure, and recommend them to families for at-home reading. (Find digital versions at scholastic.com /superreaderresources.) And, of course, supplement these lists with your own discoveries. Good luck and happy reading!

BELONGING

Grades K–2

A Birthday Basket for Tia by Pat Mora
A Path of Stars by Anne Sibley O'Brien
A Special Day by Anne Sibley O'Brien
Baseball Saved Us by Ken Mochizuki
Bigmama's by Donald Crews
Blackout by John Rocco
Chato's Kitchen by Gary Soto
Chicken Sunday by Patricia Polacco
Crow Boy by Taro Yashima
For You Are a Kenyan Child by Kelly Cunnane
Giraffes Can't Dance by Giles Andreae
Grandma's Gift by Eric Velasquez
Grandma's Records by Eric Velasquez
Hairs/Pelitos by Sandra Cisneros
Happy Pig Day! by Mo Willems
I Make Clay Pots by Leslie Johnson
I'm New Here by Anne Sibley O'Brien
Ish by Peter Reynolds
Kitchen Dance by Maurie J. Manning
Kunu's Basket by Lee DeCora Francis
Let's Talk About Race by Julius Lester
Library Lion by Michelle Knudsen
Mice and Beans by Pam Muñoz Ryan
My Brother Charlie by Holly Robinson Peete
My Name Is Yoon by Helen Recorvits
My People by Langston Hughes

Night on the Neighborhood Street by Eloise Greenfield
Nina Bonita by Ana Maria Machado
One Family by George Shannon
One World One Day by Barbara Kerley
Rosie Goes to Preschool by Karen Katz
Skit-scat Raggedy Cat by Roxane Orgill
Spoon by Amy Krouse Rosenthal
Stellaluna by Janell Cannon
The Colors of Us by Karen Katz
The Hello, Goodbye Window by Norton Juster
The New Small Person by Lauren Child
The Peace Book by Todd Parr
Too Many Tamales by Gary Soto
'Twas Nochebuena by Roseanne Greenfield Thong
Two Sweet Peas by Andria Warmflash Rosenbaum
Violet's Music by Angela Johnson
Zen Ties by Jon J. Muth

Grades 3–5

Auntie Yang's Great Soybean Picnic by Ginnie Lo
Baseball in April and Other Stories by Gary Soto
Because of Winn-Dixie by Kate DiCamillo
Brown Honey in Broomwheat Tea by Joyce Carol Thomas
Bud, Not Buddy by Christopher Paul Curtis

Calling the Doves/El Canto de las Palomas by Juan Herrera
Crow Call by Lois Lowry
Dream Big: Michael Jordan and the Pursuit of Olympic Gold by Deloris Jordan
Drita, My Homegirl by Jenny Lombard
Duke Ellington: The Piano Prince and His Orchestra by Andrea Davis Pinkney
El Deafo by Cece Bell
Going Home, Coming Home by Truong Tran
Hound Dog True by Linda Urban
Little Pink Pup by Johanna Kerby
Local News by Gary Soto
Maya's Blanket by Monica Brown
Moon Runner by Carolyn Marsden
My Brother Charlie by Holly Robinson Peete and Ryan Elizabeth Peete
Safe at Home by Mike Lupica
Strawberry Hill by Mary Hoberman
Tar Beach by Faith Ringgold
Testing the Ice by Sharon Robinson
The Birchbark House by Louise Erdrich
The Bully from the Black Lagoon by Mike Thaler
The Flag of Childhood: Poems from the Middle East by Naomi Shihab Nye
The Junkyard Wonders by Patricia Polacco
The Misadventures of the Family Fletcher by Dana Alison Levy
The Year of the Dog by Grace Lin
This Child, Every Child: A Book About the World's Children by David J. Smith

Tsunami! by Kimiko Kajikawa

Wise at Heart: Children and Adults Share Words of Wisdom by Richard Steckel

Grades 6–8

Another Day by David Levithan

Baseball Is… by Louise Borden

Blob by Frieda Wishinsky

Bluish by Virginia Hamilton

Brian's Return by Gary Paulsen

Drama by Raina Telgemeier

Fish in a Tree by Lynda Mullaly Hunt

Fitting In by Anilu Bernardo

Fresh Off the Boat by Eddie Huang

"Guess What" by Susan Noyes Anderson

I Funny: A Middle School Story by James Patterson

If a Tree Falls at Lunch Period by Gennifer Choldenko

Little Green: Growing Up During the Chinese Cultural Revolution by Chun Yu

"May Our Friendship Last Forever" by Nicholas Gordon

My Darling, My Hamburger by Paul Zindel

Persepolis: The Story of a Childhood by Marjane Satrapi

Roots and Wings by Many Ly

"She Is a Friend of Mind" by Toni Morrison

The Battle of Jericho by Sharon M. Draper

"The Glory of Friendship" by Ralph Waldo Emerson

The House on Mango Street by Sandra Cisneros

The Lions of Little Rock by Kristin Levine

The Running Dream by Wendelin Van Draanen

The Unforgotten Coat by Frank Cottrell Boyce

Unusual Chickens for the Exceptional Poultry Farmer by Kelly Jones

"Where I Am From" by George Ella Lyon

Wonder by R. J. Palacio

CURIOSITY

Grades K–2

A Weed Is a Flower: The Life of George Washington Carver by Aliki

Abuela by Arthur Dorros

Boy, Were We Wrong About Dinosaurs! by Kathleen V. Kudlinski

Call Me Tree by Maya Christina Gonzales

Chameleons Are Cool by Martin Jenkins

Copper by Kazu Kibuishi

Dear World by Takayo Nado

Diary of a Fly by Doreen Cronin

Dumpling Soup by Jama Kim Rattigan

Everybody Cooks Rice by Norah Dooley

Gotta Go! Gotta Go! by Sam Swope

Grandpa Green by Lane Smith

Guyku: A Year of Haiku for Boys by Bob Raczka

Hello Ocean by Pam Muñoz Ryan

Juna's Jar by Jane Bahk

La Mariposa by Simon Silva

Lift the Flap: Questions & Answers About Animals by Katie Daynes

Lola Loves Stories by Anna McQuinn

My Big Rock by Phyllis J. Perry

Not a Box by Antoinette Portis

On a Beam of Light by Jennifer Berne

Penguins (Seedlings) by Kate Riggs

Ramadan Moon by Na'ima Robert

Roxaboxen by Alice McLerran

Seven Blind Mice by Ed Young

Sleeping Cutie by Andrea Davis Pinkney

The Day the Crayons Quit by Drew Daywalt

The Mouse and the Meadow by Chad Wallace

The Rainbow Mystery by Jennifer Dussling

This Is the Rope: A Story From the Great Migration by Jacqueline Woodson

Tuesday by David Weisner

Weird Sea Creatures by Laura Marsh

Wemberly Worried by Kevin Henkes

What Do You Do With a Tail Like This? by Steve Jenkins and Robin Page

What If You Had Animal Hair? by Sandra Markle

What If You Had Animal Teeth? by Sandra Markle

When the Wind Stops by Charlotte Zolotow

Grades 3–5

A Light in the Attic by Shel Silverstein

Abe Lincoln's Dream by Lane Smith

All the Wild Wonders by Wendy Cooling

Bartholomew Biddle and the Very Big Wind by Gary Ross

Baseball in April and Other Stories by Gary Soto

Bayou Magic by Jewell Parker Rhodes

How & Why Stories by Martha Hamilton

How Strong Is It? by Ben Hillman

If the World Were a Village: A Book About the World's People, Second Edition, by David J. Smith

If You Lived Here: Houses of the World by Giles Laroche

If You're Not Here, Please Raise Your Hand by Kalli Dakos

Nic Bishop: Lizards by Nic Bishop

Salsa Stories by Lulu Delacre

Sky Color by Peter Reynolds

The Island of Dr. Libris by Chris Grabenstein

The Sixty-Eight Rooms by Marianne Malone

The Three Questions by Jon J. Muth

The View From the Cherry Tree by Willo Davis Roberts

The Wonder Book by Amy Krouse Rosenthal

Weslandia by Paul Fleischman

When the Beat Was Born: DJ Kool Herc and the Creation of Hip Hop by Laban Carrick Hill

Where the Mountain Meets the Moon by Grace Lin

Grades 6–8

47 by Walter Mosley

A Really Short History of Nearly Everything by Bill Bryson

Being by Kevin Brooks

Dark Shimmer by Donna Jo Napoli

Dreaming in Indian by Lisa Charleyboy and Mary Leatherdale

Holes by Louis Sachar

Incarceron by Catherine Fisher

Iqbal by Francesco D'Adamo

Moxie and the Art of Rule Breaking by Erin Dionne

One Plus One Equals Blue by M. J. Auch

Rose Blanche by Christope Gallaz

Sammy Keyes and the Hotel Thief by Wendelin Van Draanen

Soul Looks Back in Wonder by Tom Feelings

The Evolution of Calpurnia Tate by Jacqueline Kelly

To Kill a Mockingbird by Harper Lee

The Secret Garden by Frances Hodgson Burnett

The Tree of Life by Peter Sís

Unstoppable Octobia May by Sharon Flake

Wonder by R. J. Palacio

FRIENDSHIP

Grades K–2

Amos and Boris by William Steig

Bad Apple: A Tale of Friendship by Edward Hemingway

Ballet Cat the Totally Secret Secret by Bob Shea

Beauty and the Beast by H. Chuku Lee and Pat Cummings

Big Al by Andrew Clements

Crazy Hair Day by Barney Saltzberg

Diary of a Spider by Doreen Cronin

Fish Is Fish by Leo Lionni

Four Feet, Two Sandals by Karen Lynn Williams

How to Grow a Friend by Sara Gillingham

Madlenka by Peter Sís

Mango, Abuela, and Me by Meg Medina

Maria Had a Little Llama / María Tenía Una Llamita by Angela Dominguez

Mrs. Katz and Tush by Patricia Polacco

My Friend Rabbit by Eric Rohmann

New Day, New Friends by C. Alexander London

Ninja Bunny by Jennifer Gray Olson

Not Norman: A Goldfish Story by Kelly Bennett

Rainbow Joe and Me by Maria Diaz Strom

Raising Dragons by Jerdine Nolen

Rufus the Writer by Elizabeth Bram and Chuck Groenink

Sitti's Secrets by Naomi Shihab Nye

Surprise Moon by Caroline Hatton

Teammates by Peter Golenbock

The Friendly Four by Eloise Greenfield

The Gift of Nothing by Patrick McDonnell

The Mouse and the Lion by Jerry Pinkney

The Name Jar by Yangsook Choi

Those Shoes by Maribeth Boelts

Today I Will Fly! by Mo Willems

We Can Get Along: A Child's Book of Choices by Lauren Murphy Payne

When Pigasso Met Mootisse by Nina Laden

Yo! Yes? by Chris Raschka

Z Is for Moose by Kelly Bingham

Grades 3–5

Charlotte's Web by E. B. White

Clever Trevor by Sarah Albee

Dancing Home by Alma Flor Ada

Dear Mr. Henshaw by Beverly Cleary

Freedom Summer by Deborah Wiles

James and the Giant Peach by Roald Dahl

Lucky Dog: Twelve Tales of Rescued Dogs by Various Authors

Matthew and Tilly by Rebecca Jones

"May Our Friendship Last Forever" by Nicholas Gordon

My Man Blue by Nikki Grimes

Owen & Mzee: The True Story of a Remarkable Friendship by Craig Hatkoff, et al.

"The Glory of Our Friendship" by Ralph Waldo Emerson

The Madman of Piney Woods by Christopher Paul Curtis

The Misadventures of the Family Fletcher by Dana Alison Levy

The One and Only Ivan by Katherine Applegate

The Other Side by Jacqueline Woodson

The World's Greatest Elephant by Ralph Helfer

True Tales of Animal Heroes by Allan Zullo

Tua and the Elephant by R. P. Harris

Two Bobbies by Kirby Larson

Grades 6–8

Anya's Ghost by Vera Brosgol

Aquamarine and Indigo by Alice Hoffman

Because of Winn-Dixie by Kate DiCamillo

Bull Catcher by Alden R. Carter

Crash by Jerry Spinelli

Doll Bones by Holly Black

Duke by Kirby Larson

Fast Sam, Cool Clyde, and Stuff by Walter Dean Myers

Finding Audrey by Sophie Kinsella

Flip-Flop Girl by Katherine Paterson

Goodbye Stranger by Rebecca Stead

Hey World, Here I Am! by Jean Little

Holes by Louis Sachar

If a Tree Falls at Lunch by Gennifer Choldenko

I Will Always Write Back by Martin Ganda, Caitlin Alifirenka and Liz Welch

Keeping the Moon by Sarah Dessen

Kira-Kira by Cynthia Kadohata

Navigating Early by Clare Vanderpool

Night Hoops by Carl Deuker

"She Is a Friend of Mind" by Toni Morrison

Shug by Jenny Han

Sula by Toni Morrison

The Boy and the Samurai by Erik Christian Haugaard

The Kind of Friends We Used to Be by Frances O'Roark Dowell

The Kite Fighters by Linda Sue Park

The Schwa Was Here by Neal Shusterman

This Is Just to Say: Poems of Apology and Forgiveness by Joyce Sidman

Zero Tolerance by Claudia Mills

KINDNESS

Grades K–2

14 Cows for America by Carmen Agra Deedy

Anna Hibiscus by Atinuke

Big Red Lollipop by Rukhsana Khan

Bossy Gallito/El gallo de bodas by Lucia M. Gonzalez

Chrysanthemum by Kevin Henkes

Clara and Davie by Patricia Polacco

Each Kindness by Jacqueline Woodson

Frog and Toad All Year by Arnold Lobel

Horton Hears a Who! by Dr. Seuss

I Broke My Trunk! by Mo Willems

I Want My Hat Back by Jon Klassen

Mice and Beans by Pam Muñoz Ryan

Miss Rumphius by Barbara Cooney

Neville by Norton Juster

Peaceful Pieces by Anna Grossnickle Hines

Pierre the Penguin by Jean Marzollo

Plant a Kiss by Amy K. Rosenthal

Sukey and the Mermaid by Robert D. San Souci

The Invisible Boy by Trudy Ludwig

Wanda's Roses by Pat Brisson

Willow by Denise Brennan-Nelson and Rosemarie Brennan

Wings by Christopher Myers

You Should Can a Friend by Tony and Lauren Dungy

Z Is for Moose by Kelly Bingham

Grades 3–5

"By Myself" by Eloise Greenfield

Charlotte's Web by E. B. White

"Don't Quit" by Anonymous

Everything Pets: Furry Facts, Photos, and Fun—Unleashed! by James Spears

It Jes' Happened: When Bill Traylor Started to Draw by Don Tate

Mr. Lincoln's Way by Patricia Polacco

Mufaro's Beautiful Daughters by John Steptoe

No Talking by Andrew Clements

Passage to Freedom: The Sugihara Story by Ken Mochizuki

Peaceful Pieces by Anna Grossnickle Hines

President of the Whole Fifth Grade by Sherri Winston

Profiles #6: Peace Warriors by Andrea Davis Pinkney

Sparrow Girl by Sara Pennypacker

Sukey and the Mermaid by Robert D. San Souci

The Crane Wife by Odds Bodkin

The Dog Who Loved Tortillas / La perrita que le encantaban las tortillas by Benjamin Alire Sáenz

The Honest-to-Goodness Truth by Patricia McKissack

"The Invitation" by Shel Silverstein

The Penderwicks: A Summer Tale of Four Sisters, Two Rabbits, and a Very Interesting Boy by Jeanne Birdsall

The Quiltmaker's Journey by Jeff Brumbeau

The Tale of Despereaux by Kate DiCamillo

The Three Questions by Jon J. Muth

The Trees of the Dancing Goats by Patricia Polacco

The Yak, the Python, the Frog by Hilaire Belloc

Grades 6-8

Anne of Avonlea by L.M. Montgomery

Anson's Way by Gary D. Schmidt

Black Beauty by Anna Sewell

"Build a Box of Friendship" by Chuck Pool

Freak the Mighty by Rodman Philbrick

"Friends" by Anonymous

"Imagine a World" by Anonymous

Indigo's Star by Hilary McKay

Kira-Kira by Cynthia Kadohata

Little Lord Fauntleroy by Frances Hodgson Burnett

Marcelo in the Real World by Francisco Stork

Parrots Over Puerto Rico by Cindy Trumbore

Seedfolks by Paul Fleischman

The Gift of the Magi and Other Short Stories by O. Henry

The Hunchback of Notre Dame by Victor Hugo

The Laura Line by Crystal Allen

The River Between Us by Richard Peck

The Truth About Sparrows by Marian Hale

The Wednesday Wars by Gary D. Schmidt

The Women of Brewster Place by Gloria Naylor

The Young Landlords by Walter Dean Myers

William S. and the Great Escape by Zilpha Keatley Snyder

CONFIDENCE

Grades K-2

A Bad Case of Stripes by David Shannon

Alvin Ailey by Andrea Davis Pinkney

Bintou's Braids by Sylviane A. Diouf

Chester the Brave by Audrey Penn

Dancing in the Wings by Debbie Allen

Diego Rivera: His World and Ours by Duncan Tonatiuh

Dizzy by Jonah Winter

Ellie by Mike Wu

Exclamation Mark by Amy Krouse Rosenthal

Fancy Dance by Leslie Johnson

Freckle Juice by Judy Blume

Free to Be… You and Me by Marlo Thomas and Friends

Harlem's Little Blackbird by Renée Watson

I Got the Rhythm by Connie Schofield-Morrison

I Like Me! by Nancy Carlson

I Want to Be by Thylias Moss

I Wish I Were a Butterfly by James Howe

Iggy Peck, Architect by Andrea Beaty

Jingle Dancer by Cynthia Leitich Smith

Layla's Head Scarf by Miriam Cohen

Little Kunoichi, The Ninja Girl by Sanae Ishida

Marisol McDonald Doesn't Match: Marisol McDonald no combina by Monica Brown

Molly, by Golly by Dianne Ochiltree

One Hen: How One Small Loan Made a Big Difference by Katie Smith Milway

Pete the Cat and His Four Groovy Buttons by Eric Litwin

Pinduli by Janell Cannon

Salt in His Shoes: Michael Jordan in Pursuit of a Dream by Deloris Jordan and Roslin M. Jordan

Suki's Kimono by Chieri Uegaki

The Camping Trip That Changed America by Barb Rosenstock

The Dot by Peter Reynolds

Unicorn Thinks He's Pretty Great by Bob Shea

What Do You Do With an Idea? by Kobi Yamada

Whistle for Willie by Ezra Jack Keats

Whoever You Are by Mem Fox

Grades 3-5

Alice the Brave by Phyllis Naylor

Allie's Basketball Dream by Barbara E. Barber

An Eye for Color by Natasha Wing

Annabel the Actress Starring in "Gorilla My Dreams" by Ellen Conford

Better Than You by Trudy Ludwig

Bobby the Brave (Sometimes) by Lisa Yee

Broken Bike Boy and the Queen of 33rd Street by Sharon G. Flake

Bud, Not Buddy by Christopher Paul Curtis

Emmanuel's Dream: The True Story of Emmanuel Ofosu Yeboah by Laurie Ann Thompson

First Day in Grapes by L. King Pérez

Found Things by Marilyn Hilton

Funny Bones: Posada and His Day of the Dead Calaveras by Duncan Tonatiuh

Girl Wonder: A Baseball Story in Nine Innings by Deborah Hopkinson

Hardcourt Comeback by Fred Bowen

Home Court by Amar'e Stoudemire

Indian Shoes by Cynthia Leitich Smith

Joshua's Masai Mask by Dakari Hru

Just Like Josh Gibson by Angela Johnson

Knots on a Counting Rope by Bill Martin Jr.

Long Shot by Chris Paul

Looking Like Me by Walter Dean Myers

My Name Is Maria Isabel by Alma Flor Ada

Nightbird by Alice Hoffman

She Loved Baseball: The Effa Manley Story by Audrey Vernick

Sonya Sotomayor: A Judge Grows in the Bronx by Jonah Winter

The Dream Keeper and Other Poems by Langston Hughes

The Gold-Threaded Dress by Carolyn Marsden

The Million Dollar Kick by Dan Gutman

The Missing Piece by Shel Silverstein

Grades 6-8

A Game for Swallows: To Die, to Leave, to Return by Zeina Abirached

American Born Chinese by Gene Luen Yang

Bayou Magic by Jewell Parker Rhodes

Brown Girl Dreaming by Jacqueline Woodson

Call Me Maria by Judith Ortiz Cofer

Call on the Stars by Sally Prue

Fly High! The Story of Bessie Coleman by Louise Borden and Mary Kay Kroeger

Full Cicada Moon by Marilyn Hilton

Hoot by Carl Hiaasen

How Lamar's Bad Prank Won a Bubba-Sized Trophy by Crystal Allen

How Tia Lola Came to (Visit) Stay by Julia Alvarez

Lion Boy by Zizou Corder

Little Women by Louisa May Alcott

Out of My Mind by Sharon Draper

Poetry Speaks: Who I Am edited by Elise Paschen

Rad American Women A-Z by Kate Schatz

Silhouetted by the Blue by Traci L. Jones

Spider Boy by Ralph Fletcher

Squashed by Joan Bauer

Storm Thief by Chris Wooding

The Girl at the Center of the World by Austin Aslan

The Green Bicycle by Haifaa Al Mansour

The Hunger Games by Suzanne Collins

The Red Pencil by Andrea Davis Pinkney

Throwing Shadows by E.L. Konigsburg

Travel Team by Mike Lupica

Truth and Salsa by Linda Lowery

While I Live by John Marsden

Winner Takes All by Jenny Santana

COURAGE

Grades K–2

Abiyoyo by Pete Seeger

Anansi Goes Fishing by Janet Stevens

Doctor De Soto by William Steig

Doña Flor by Pat Mora

Fire! Fuego! Brave Bomberos by Susan Middleton Elya

Gordon Parks by Carole Boston Weatherford

Gregory's Shadow by Don Freeman

I Am Jackie Robinson by Brad Meltzer

Jackie Robinson by Wil Mara

Lakas and the Makibaka Hotel by Anthony Robles

Let's Play in the Forest While the Wolf Is Not Around by Claudia Rueda

Let's Read About… César Chávez by Jerry Tello

Lillian's Right to Vote by Jonah Winter

Loud Emily by Alexis O'Neill

Louder, Lili by Gennifer Choldenko

Niño Wrestles the World by Yuyi Morales

Orion and the Dark by Emma Yarlett

Precious and the Boo Hag by Patricia McKissack

Roberto: The Insect Architect by Nina Laden

Scaredy Squirrel by Melanie Watt

Sheila Rae, the Brave by Kevin Henkes

Sit-In: How Four Friends Stood Up by Sitting Down by Andrea Davis Pinkney

Sophie's Masterpiece by Eileen Spinelli

Stand Tall Molly Lou Melon by Patty Lovell

Swimmy by Leo Lionni

The Hating Book by Charlotte Zolotow

The Ogre Bully by Aaron Hoffmire

The Secret Shortcut by Mark Teague

The Story of Ruby Bridges by Robert Coles

The Very Busy Spider by Eric Carle

Two of a Kind by Jacqui Robbins

Viva Frida by Yuyi Morales

Grades 3–5

A Boy Called Slow by Joseph Bruchac

Antonio's Card (La Tarjeta de Antonio) by Rigoberto Gonzales

Azzi in Between by Sarah Garland

Beautiful Warrior by Emily Arnold McCully

Chains by Laurie Halse Anderson

Fuzzy Mud by Louis Sachar

Hank Aaron: Brave in Every Way by Peter Golenblock

Heat by Mike Lupica

Hereville: How Mirka Got Her Sword by Barry Deutsch

Heroes by Ken Mochizuki

Jim's Lion by Russell Hoban

Life Doesn't Frighten Me by Maya Angelou

Long Shot by Mike Lupica

Moonshot by Brian Floca

Pink and Say by Patricia Polacco

Planting the Trees of Kenya by Claire A. Nivola

Queen of the Falls by Chris Van Allsburg

Roll of Thunder, Hear My Cry by Mildred Taylor

Ron's Big Mission by Rose Blue

Sojourner Truth's Step-Stomp Stride by Andrea Davis Pinkney

The Chalk Box Kid by Clyde Robert Bulla

The Closet Ghosts by Uma Krishnaswami

The Dreamer by Pam Muñoz Ryan

The Hundred Dresses by Eleanor Estes

The Hunterman and the Crocodile by Baba Wagué Diakité

The Jumbies by Tracey Baptiste

The Mud Pony by Caron Lee Cohen

The Reluctant Dragon by Kenneth Grahame

Tiger Boy by Mitali Perkins

When Marian Sang by Pam Muñoz Ryan

Zita the Spacegirl by Ben Hatke

Grades 6–8

A Long Walk to Water by Linda Sue Park

A Single Shard by Linda Sue Park

A Time to Dance by Padma Venkatraman

Beardance by Will Hobbs

Before We Were Free by Julia Alvarez

"Black Eye Ball" by Steve Micciche

Box Out by John Coy

Boys Without Names by Kashmira Sheth

Bright Shadow by Avi

Call It Courage by Armstrong Sperry

Chasing Secrets by Gennifer Choldenko

Courage for Beginners by Karen Harrington

Esperanza Rising by Pam Muñoz Ryan

Gaby, Lost and Found by Ángela Cervantes

Helen Keller by Langston Hughes

I Survived Book Series 1–6 by Lauren Tarshis

Just Juice by Karen Hesse

My Side of the Mountain by Jean Craighead George

Okay for Now by Gary D. Schmidt

Public School Superhero by James Patterson

Real Kids, Real Stories, Real Change: Courageous Actions Around the World by Garth Sundem

Serafina and the Black Cloak by Robert Beatty

Shadowshaper by Daniel José Older

Stargirl by Jerry Spinelli

Stella by Starlight by Sharon Draper

The Living by Matt de la Pena

The Misfits by James Howe *The River* by Gary Paulsen

The Safest Lie by Angela Cerrito

The Watsons Go to Birmingham—1963 by Christopher Paul Curtis

Up From the Sea by Leza Lowitz

HOPE

Grade K-2

A Chair for My Mother by Vera B. Williams

A Dance Like Starlight: One Ballerina's Dream by Kristy Dempsey

A Home for Bird by Philip C. Stead

A Splash of Red: The Art and Life of Horace Pippin by Jennifer Fisher Bryant

Allie's Basketball Dream by Barbara E. Barber

Book Fiesta! by Pat Mora

Bring Me Some Apples and I'll Make You a Pie by Robbin Gourley

Bucket Filling from A–Z by Carol McCloud

Come on, Rain! by Karen Hesse

Dreaming Up by Christy Hale

Eight Days: A Story of Haiti by Edwidge Danticat

Fifty Cents and a Dream: Young Booker T. Washington by Jabari Asim

Fly Away Home by Eve Bunting

Fly Free! by Rosanne Thong

Gleam and Glow by Eve Bunting

Happy Birthday, Martin Luther King Jr. by Jean Marzollo

Hawk, I'm Your Brother by Byrd Baylor

Honey, I Love and Other Love Poems by Eloise Greenfield

If a Bus Could Talk by Faith Ringgold

Little Blue and Little Yellow by Leo Lionni

Little Melba and Her Big Trombone by Katheryn Russell-Brown

Max Found Two Sticks by Brian Pinkney

Miss Rumphius by Barbara Cooney

Perfect Square by Michael Hall

Ruby's Wish by Shirin Yim Bridges

Sing by Tom Lichtenheld and Joe Raposo

Steam Train, Dream Train by Sherri Duskey Rinker and Tom Lichtenheld

Stone Soup by Jon J. Muth

The Great Migration by Eloise Greenfield

The Green Mother Goose: Saving the World One Rhythm at a Time by David Davis and Jan Peck

The People Could Fly by Virginia Hamilton

The Pigeon Wants a Puppy! by Mo Willems

The Tree Lady by H. Joseph Hopkins

Tito Puente Mambo King by Monica Brown

Train to Somewhere by Eve Bunting

We Are Alike, We Are Different by Janice Behrens

Grades 3–5

31 Ways to Change the World by We Are What We Do

A Nation's Hope: The Story of Boxing Legend Joe Louis by Matt de la Pena

Alexander and the Terrible, Horrible, No Good, Very Bad Day by Judith Viorst

Brothers in Hope: The Story of the Lost Boys of Sudan by Mary Williams

Child of the Civil Rights Movement by Paula Young Shelton and Raúl Colón

Crossing Bok Chitto: A Choctaw Tale of Friendship and Freedom by Tim Tingle

Dear Malala, We Stand With You by Rosemary McCarney

Firebird by Misty Copeland

Harvesting Hope: The Story of Cesar Chavez by Kathleen Krull

Henry's Freedom Box by Ellen Levine

Hidden: A Child's Story of the Holocaust by Greg Salsedo and Loïc Dauvillier

Hope for Winter by David Yates, Craig Hatkoff, Juliana Hatkoff, and Isabella Hatkoff

How You Got So Smart by David Milgrim

I Can Make a Difference by Marian Wright Edelman

I Have a Dream by Martin Luther King, Jr.

I, Too, Am America by Langston Hughes

Josephine: The Dazzling Life of Josephine Baker by Patricia Hruby Powell

Little Red Writing by Joan Holub

March On! The Day My Brother Martin Changed the World by Christine King Farris

Martin's Big Words by Doreen Rappaport

Miss Todd and Her Wonderful Flying Machine Kristina Yee and Frances Poletti

Nelson Mandela by Kadir Nelson

Poetry for Young People: Langston Hughes by David Roessel

Ruth and the Green Book by Calvin Alexander Ramsey

Silent Music: A Story of Baghdad by James Rumford

The Harmonica by Tony Johnston

The Secret Message by Mina Javaherbin

Toothpaste Millionaire by Jean Merrill

Where the Sidewalk Ends by Shel Silverstein

Wilma Unlimited by Kathleen Krull

Grades 6–8

Bad Boy by Walter Dean Myers

Bird by Angela Johnson

Bird in a Box by Andrea Davis Pinkney

Bull Rider by Suzanne Morgan Williams

Confetti Girl by Diana López

Counting by 7s by Holly Goldberg Sloan

Echo by Pam Muñoz Ryan

Hana's Suitcase by Karen Levine

I Am Malala by Malala Yousafzai

Inside Out and Back Again by Thanhha Lai

Jesse by Gary Soto

Journey of the Sparrows by Fran Leeper Buss

Journey Through Heartsongs by Mattie J. T. Stepanek

La Linea by Ann Jaramillo

Long Journey Home by Julius Lester

Letters from a Slave Girl: The Story of Harriet Jacobs by Mary E. Lyons

Mare's War by Tanita S. Davis

Milkweed by Jerry Spinelli

No Turning Back by Beverley Naidoo

One Crazy Summer by Rita Williams-Garcia

Poached by Stuart Gibbs

Ruby Lee & Me by Shannon Hitchcock

Rules for Stealing Stars by Corey Ann Haydu

Shooting the Moon by Frances Dowell

Stitches: A Memoir by David Small

The Boy Who Harnessed the Wind by William Kamkwamba and Bryan Mealer

The Thing About Luck by Cynthia Kadohata

There Are No Children Here by Alex Kotlowitz

Where the Mountain Meets the Moon by Grace Lin

Professional References Cited

ACT (2014). The condition of college & career readiness 2013: Hispanic students. Retrieved from http://www.act.org/newsroom/data/2013/states/hispanic.html

Agar, M. (1994). Language shock: Understanding the culture of conversation. New York, NY: Morrow.

Allington, R. L., & Gabriel, R. E. (2012, March). Every child, every day. *Educational Leadership*. The Association of Supervision and Curriculum Development (ASCD), *69*(6).

Allington, R. L., and McGill-Franzen, A. (2013). *Summer reading: Closing the rich/poor achievement gap*. New York, NY: Teachers College Press.

Allington, R. L. (2002). What I've learned about effective reading instruction from a decade of studying exemplary elementary classroom teachers. *Phi Delta Kappan, 83*(10), 740–747.

Allington, R. L, McCuiston, K., & Billen, M. (2015). What research says about text complexity and learning to read. *The Reading Teacher, 68*(7), 491–501.

Anderson, R. C., Hiebert, E. H., Scott, J. A., & Wilkinson, I. A. G. (1985). *Becoming a nation of readers: The report of the Commission on Reading*. Washington, DC: National Institute of Education.

Anderson, R. C., Wilson, P. T., & Fielding, L. G. (1988). Growth in reading and how children spend their time outside of school. *Reading Research Quarterly, 23*(3), 285–303.

Atwell, N. (2014). *In the middle: A lifetime of learning about writing, reading, and adolescents* (3rd ed). Portsmouth, NH: Heinemann.

Beers, K. (2003). *When kids can't read: What teachers can do*. Portsmouth, NH: Heinemann.

Bergin, C., & Bergin, D. (2009). Attachment in the classroom. *Educational Psychology Review, 21*, 141–170.

Bishop, R. S. (1990). Mirrors, window, and sliding glass doors. *Perspectives, 6*(3), ix-xi.

Blachowicz, C., & Fisher, P. (2015). Best practices in vocabulary instruction. In L. Gambrell & L. M. Morrow (Eds.), *Best practices in literacy instruction* (5th ed.) (pp. 195–222). New York, NY: Guilford Press.

Bowlby, J. (1969). *Attachment (Vol 1)*. New York, NY: Basic Books.

Braxton, B. (2007). Developing your reading-aloud skills. *Teacher Librarian, 34*(4), 56–57, 68.

California Department of Education. (2015). *English language arts/English language development framework for California public schools: Kindergarten through grade twelve*. Sacramento, CA: California Department of Education.

Cazden, C. (1988). *Classroom discourse: The language of teaching and learning*. Portsmouth, NH: Heinemann.

Center on the Developing Child at Harvard University. (2015). *Supportive relationships and active skill-building strengthen the foundations of resilience: Working paper 13*. Retrieved from www.developingchild.harvard.edu

Culham, R. (2010). *Traits of writing: The complete guide for middle school*. New York, NY: Scholastic.

Cullinan, B. E. (2000). Independent reading and school achievement. *School Library Media Research, 3*, 1–23.

Cunningham, A. E., & Stanovich, K. E. (1998, Spring/Summer). What reading does for the mind. *American Educator*, 8–17.

Cunningham, A. E., & Zibulsky, J. (2014). *Book smart: How to develop and support successful, motivated readers*. Oxford, England: Oxford University Press.

Currie, L. (2014, October 17). Why teaching kindness in schools is essential to reduce bullying. [Blog post]. Retrieved from http://www.edutopia.org/blog/teaching-kindness-essential-reduce-bullying-lisa-currie

DeCasper, A. J., & Spence, M. (1986). Prenatal maternal speech influences newborns' perception of speech sounds. *Infant Behavior and Development, 9*(2), 133–150.

Diener, E., & Seligman, M. E. P. (2002). Very happy people. *Psychological Science, 13*, 80–83.

Djikic, M., Oatley, K., & Moldoveanu, M. (2013). Reading other minds: Effects of literature on empathy. *Scientific Study of Literature, 3*(1), 28–47.

Duke, N. (2014). *Inside information: Developing powerful readers and writers through project-based instruction*. New York, NY: Scholastic.

Duke, N., & Martin, N. (2015). Best practices in informational text comprehension instruction. In L. Gambrell & L. M. Morrow (Eds.), *Best practices in literacy instruction* (5th ed.) (pp. 249–267). New York, NY: Guilford Press.

Dyson, A. H. (1995). The courage to write: Child meaning making in a contested world. *Language Arts, 72*(5), 324–333.

Eccles, J. S., & Wigfield, A. (2002). Motivational beliefs, values, and goals. *Annual Review of Psychology, 53*, 109–132.

Edmundson, M. (2015). *Self and soul: A defense of ideals*. Cambridge, MA: Harvard University Press.

Education Week. (2012, June 7). Diplomas Count 2012: Trailing behind, moving forward: Latino students in U.S. schools. Retrieved from http://www.edweek.org/ew/toc/2012/06/07/

Engel, S. (2015). *The hungry mind: The origins of curiosity in childhood*. Cambridge, MA: Harvard University Press.

Evans, M., Kelley, J., Sikorac, J., & Treimand, D. (2010). Family scholarly culture and educational success: books and schooling in 27 nations. *Research in Social Stratification and Mobility, 28*, 171–197.

Fisher, D., Flood, J., Lapp, D., & Frey, N. (2004). Interactive read alouds: Is there a common set of implementation practices? *The Reading Teacher, 58*, 8–17.

Freire, P. (1970). *Pedagogy of the oppressed*. New York, NY: Continuum.

Gallup. (2014). Postsecondary education aspirations and barriers. Washington, DC: Gallup Inc.

Gates, B. (2000). *Business @ the speed of thought: Succeeding in the digital economy*. New York, NY: Penguin.

Ginwright, S. (2015). *Hope and healing in urban education: How urban activists and teachers are reclaiming matters of the heart*. New York, NY: Routledge.

Goleman, D. (2011). *Leadership: The power of emotional intelligence*. Florence, MA: More Than Sound.

Graham, S., & Hebert, M. (2010). Writing to read: A meta-analysis of the impact of writing and writing instruction on reading. *Harvard Educational Review, 81*(4).

Graham, S., & Perin, D. (2007). *Writing next: Effective strategies to improve writing of adolescents in middle and high schools: A report to the Carnegie Corporation of New York*. Washington, DC: Alliance for Excellent Education.

Guthrie, J. (2004). Teaching for literacy engagement. *Journal of Literacy Research, 36*(1), 1–30.

Guthrie, J. T., & Greaney, V. (1991). Literacy acts. In R. Barr, M. L. Kamil, P. Mosenthal, & P. D. Pearson (Eds.), Handbook of reading research, Vol. II (pp. 68–96). New York, NY: Longman.

Harvard Business Review. (2014, August 27). Curiosity is as important as intelligence. Retrieved from https://hbr.org/2014/08/curiosity-is-as-important-as-intelligence/

Heard, G. (2016). *Heart maps: Helping students create and craft authentic writing.* Portsmouth, NH: Heinemann.

Hiebert, E. H., & Reutzel, D. R. (Eds.). (2010). *Revisiting silent reading: New directions for teachers and researchers.* Newark, DE: International Reading Association.

Hutton, J. S., Horowitz-Kraus, T., Mendelsohn A. L., DeWitt, T., & Holland, S. K. (2015). Home reading environment and brain activation in preschool children listening to stories. *Pediatrics, 136*(3), 466–478.

Johnson, D., & Blair, A. (2003). The importance and use of student self-selected literature to reading engagement in an elementary reading curriculum. *Reading Horizons, 43*(3), 181–202.

Kalb, G., & van Ours, J. C. (2013). *Reading to young children: A head-start in life?* Melbourne, Australia: The Melbourne Institute of Applied Economic and Social Research. Working Paper No. 17/13. Retrieved from https://www.melbourneinstitute.com/downloads/working_paper_series/wp2013n17.pdf

Kidd, D. C., and Castano, E. (2013). Reading literary fiction improves theory of mind. *Science, 342*(6156), 377–380.

Krashen, S. D. (2004). *The power of reading: Insights From the research.* Santa Barbara, CA: Libraries Unlimited.

Lesesne, T. S. (2006). Reading aloud: A worthwhile investment? *Voices From the Middle, 13*(4), 50–54.

Lewis, C. (2001). *Literary practices as social acts: Power, status, and cultural norms in the classroom.* Mahwah, NJ: Lawrence Erlbaum Associates, Inc.

Miller, D. (2009). *The book whisperer: Awakening the inner reader in every child.* San Francisco, CA: Jossey-Bass.

Moje, E. B., Overby, M., Tysvaer, N., & Morris, K. (2008). The complex world of adolescent literacy: Myths, motivations, and mysteries. *Harvard Educational Review, 78*(1), 107–154.

National Scientific Council on the Developing Child. (2015). Supportive relationships and active skill-building strengthen the foundations of resilience: working paper 13. Retrieved from http://developingchild.harvard.edu/resources/supportive-relationships-and-active-skill-building-strengthen-the-foundations-of-resilience/

Noddings, N. (2003). *Happiness and education.* Cambridge, UK: Cambridge University Press.

O'Grady, P. (2012, October 26). Positive psychology in the classroom. friendship: The key to happiness.[Blog post]. Retrieved from https://www.psychologytoday.com/blog/positive-psychology-in-the-classroom/201210/friendship-the-key-happiness

Paul, A. M. (2012, March). Your brain on fiction. Retrieved from http://www.nytimes.com/2012/03/18/opinion/sunday/the-neuroscience-of-your-brain-on-fiction.html?_r=0

Pelkey, L. (2013). In the LD Bubble. In M. Adams, W. Blumenfeld, C. Castaneda, H. Hackman, M. Peters, & and X. Zuniga (Eds.), (3rd ed.) *Reading for Diversity and Social Justice.* New York, NY: Routledge.

Reardon, S. F. (2011). The widening academic achievement gap between the rich and the poor: New evidence and possible explanations. In G. J. Duncan & R. J. Murnane, (Eds.), *Whither opportunity? Rising inequality, schools, and children's life chances* (91–117). New York, NY: The Russell Sage Foundation.

Rittner, C., & Myers, S. (Eds.) (1989). *The courage to care.* New York, NY: NYU Press.

Rowe, D., Fain, J. G., & Fink, L. (2013). The family backpack project: Responding to dual-language texts through family journals. *Language Arts, 90*(6), 402–416.

Rumberger, R. (2011). *Dropping out: Why kids drop out of high school and what can be done about it.* Cambridge, MA: Harvard University Press.

Schaps, E. (March/April 2009). Creating caring school communities. *Leadership,* 8–11.

Scholastic Inc. (2015). *Kids & Family Reading Report, Fifth Edition.* New York, NY: Scholastic.

Selman, R. (2007). *The promotion of social awareness: Powerful lessons from the partnership of developmental theory and classroom practice.* New York, NY: Russell Sage Foundation.

Smith, F. (1987). *Joining the literacy club: Further essays into education.* Portsmouth, NH: Heinemann.

Sobol, T. (2013). *My life in school.* Scarsdale, NY: Public Schools of Tomorrow.

Sotomayor, S. *Fresh Air. An Interview with Terry Gross.* National Public Radio: January 13, 2014. Web Aug. 30 2015.

Stetser, M., & Stillwell, R. (2014). *Public high school four-year on-time graduation rates and event dropout rates: School years 2010–11 and 2011–12: First Look* (NCES 2014-391). U.S. Department of Education. Washington, DC: National Center for Education Statistics. Retrieved [date] from http://nces.ed.gov/pubsearch

Sullivan, A., & Brown, M. (2013). *Social inequalities in cognitive scores at age 16: The role of reading.* London, UK: Centre for Longitudinal Studies.

Taylor, B. M., Frye, B. J., & Maruyama, G. M. (1990). Time spent reading and reading growth. *American Educational Research Journal, 27*(2), 351–362.

Trelease, J. (2006). *The Read-Aloud Handbook.* New York, NY: Penguin Group.

UNESCO Institute for Statistics (2013). *Adult and youth literacy: National, regional and global trends, 1985-2015.* Montreal, Quebec: UNESCO Institute for Statistics.

Vezzali, L., Stathi, S., Giovanni, D., Capozza, D., & Trifiletti, E. (2014). The greatest Harry Potter magic of all: Reducing prejudice. *Journal of Applied Social Psychology, 45*(2), 105–121.

Wells, G. (1989). Language in the classroom: Literacy and collaborative talk. *Language Education 3*(4), 251–273.

Wiley, T. G., & de Klerk, G. (2010). Common myths and stereotypes regarding literacy and language diversity in the multilingual United States. In M. Farr, L. Seloni, & J. Song (Eds.), *Ethnolinguistic diversity and education: Language, literacy, and culture* (pp. 23–43). New York, NY: Routledge.

Wilhelm, J. (1996). *You gotta BE the book: Teaching engaged and reflective reading with adolescents.* New York, NY: Teachers College Press.

Index